THE BEAUTY OF
TREES

THE BEAUTY OF
TREES

MICHAEL JORDAN

CONSULTANT
TONY KIRKHAM
ROYAL BOTANICAL GARDENS, KEW

Quercus

CONTENTS

INTRODUCTION

To people of bygone ages, trees were possessed of immanence, an ethos that went beyond that which is simply to be explained in terms of the tangible and material. In a mighty, timeless oak, or a vast wellingtonia, whose lifespan readily outstrips our own, great strength and permanence was perceived. Arising from roots that penetrate deep into the earth, their trunks and limbs reach out to brush the sky. Many years ago an eminent visitor, invited to give a midsummer talk at my school, addressed some surprising words to his young audience that have since taken on a more trendy vogue. He suggested that if we can be sufficiently unabashed to clasp our arms tightly around the oldest and most gnarled of trunks that we can find, there will be a change, and something remarkable will flow out of the tree akin to energy charging a battery. Romantic stuff, maybe, but his words have stayed with me, and more than ever as I grow older, I sense that to walk in a great forest is to enter into a living, breathing organism, a creature of extraordinary beauty, strength and wonder. From whence emanates this mystical engine power of trees? I lack the wisdom to answer such a question. Long ago, people who lived in more intimate contact with nature did, however, possess such insight. A great tree was imbued with a sanctity that made it precious. Its well-being mattered; its death whether by natural cause or premature felling, a rite of passage with profound importance. A spirituality was being destroyed, and thus for many in past ages not only the trees but also such implements as the woodman's axe bore their own sacred dimension. Much of this sentiment has since been stripped away from our modern and technologically-driven lives, yet each of us is probably still touched in our own private way by the spiritual strength and beauty of these extraordinary life forms.

The vestiges that are left to us of the mighty forests that once clothed the greater part of our world have rightly been described as the lungs of the Earth. We cannot survive without them because they provide much of the air that we breathe, yet perversely we seem bent on their destruction at an ever-increasing rate through an insatiable demand for the necessities of modern lving. We burn hectare upon hectare of woodland to create fresh agricultural land; we obliterate forests to manufacture paper and packing crates, floorboards, telegraph poles and designer toilet seats. Only an impoverished fraction of what we destroy is replaced by planting and this often results in sterile monocultures devoid of other forms of life that rely on trees. This book will, I hope, serve to rekindle a little of our awareness of the intrinsic beauty and irreplaceable value of trees, and the need that we should cherish them for the sake of future generations. It includes some of the loveliest of trees, but also those of indispensible ecological and material value.

The trees are arranged alphabetically by Latin names. Common names vary but Latin is a universal language for the classification of plants and animals. The species span the globe and are chosen for their fine architecture, their floral beauty, and sometimes just for quirkiness.

When a tree is described as being 'native to' a particular continent or a region of the globe, this means that it occurs there naturally. It has not been transported and planted by human hand as a cultivated alien. The term is thus synonymous with 'indigenous to'. Where measurements are given (height, trunk diameter, trunk girth and spread), we refer to the average maximum that a species will reach, though in exceptional cases this can be exceeded by particularly long-lived specimen.

GRAND FIR

Abies grandis

A mighty and elegant evergreen tree of the lowland Pacific coasts of North America, the inland Cascade Mountains and parts of central Canada east of the Great Lakes, the grand fir lives up to its name, and its crown stands head and shoulders above much of the rest of the forest canopy. It is the fastest growing of all North American firs, and in northern California it can achieve a height of over 40 metres (131 ft) in just 50 years. It is also a tree of considerable longevity, with some venerable specimens passing 300 years of age.

The geographical range of the grand fir is extensive, stretching from British Columbia in the far north to northern California. Displaying two distinct ecological variants, the coast grand fir and the interior grand fir, the variety found in the lowland coastal regions matures at about twice the speed of its counterpart, which grows on the slopes of the Cascades to an altitude of 900 metres (2,953 ft) and has rather more slender cones with thinner scales.

Like its Nordmann fir cousin in Europe, the tree is cone shaped, although the crown can become more rounded and straggly, even anvil-topped in old age. The grey bark of the trunk and the gently drooping main branches become very thick as they age, typically cracked to expose purplish-red furrows. The needles, containing a pungently aromatic resin reminiscent of turpentine, are borne in two uniform rows on the lower branches, but are spiralled and arise in single ranks towards the crown. Each needle, glossy on the upper surface with two paler stripes beneath, is flattened in cross-section and bears a little notch at the tip. Below ground the tree can be anchored by a deeply probing tap root in dry positions, but substitutes this for shallow lateral roots if ground water is readily available.

The timber is soft and pale in colour, so it is used principally in paper making, as well as for packing-crate manufacture and limited internal building work. In common with the Nordmann fir, propagation is wholly through seed dispersal. Individual male and female flowers form during summer, but then enter a dormant period over the ensuing winter; pollination does not take place until the following spring. When fertilized, the female inflorescence develops into a cone that stands erect on the branch and can be up to 12 centimetres (5 in) long, containing scaly bracts each of which bears a winged seed that is released as the bracts distintegrate and fall off, eventually leaving a central 'core' on the tree. The little seedlings, once germinated, are especially vulnerable and over 30 per cent die during the first year of growth.

GRAND FIR

Evergreen

NATIVE TO *Western and central North America*
HEIGHT *45 m (148 ft)*
TRUNK DIAMETER *2 m (7 ft)*
TRUNK GIRTH *6.25 m (21 ft)*
SPREAD *5 m (16 ft)*

ABOVE *The aromatic needles arise in little fans before settling into rows.*

LEFT *The imposing trunks of grand fir soar skywards in a forest in British Columbia, Canada.*

NORDMANN FIR

Abies nordmanniana

With its downward-sloping branches, the Nordmann fir is among the prettiest of European fir trees, so it is not entirely surprising that in recent times we have often chosen this species for Christmas, in preference to the more traditional Norway spruce. The needles are not sharp and they resist the annoying temptation to shed and carpet the floor. A native of mountainous regions of Turkey and Armenia, chiefly around the Black Sea but also extending into the Russian Caucasus, Nordmann fir was first planted in western Europe in the 1800s, where today it is often cultivated in nurseries.

Many of those growing in the western Caucasus reach truly massive proportions, easily achieving a height of 60 metres (197 ft) and acquiring a girth of up to 5 metres (16 ft). Specimen trees, however, reportedly reach even greater height, as much as 85 metres (279 ft), thus making them the tallest living things in Europe. Growing quickly in the first two or three years from seed germination, and continuing almost as rapidly, only slowing in old age, they require well-drained but moist soil with a plentiful supply of fresh water, hence they prefer life on north-facing slopes experiencing cool, wet summers. The trees can thrive at altitudes of as much as 2,000 metres (6,562 ft), but require annual rainfall of at least 1,000 millimetres (39 in). Two distinct species are recognized: the Caucasian fir and the Turkish fir, which intermingle and hybridize where they meet in northern Turkey.

The tree is broadly conical with light grey bark, and bears single evergreen needles in flat rows of two, or arranged in spirals along the branches. It can hold onto its leaves, remarkably, for up to 26 years without shedding. Scented with aromatic resin, each needle is glossy dark and green above, but underneath reveals two distinctive whitish bands of stomata or breathing pores on either side of a green midrib, or central vein.

The wood is soft, very pale in colour, and in the main it is grown commercially to be pulped for paper making. The timber possesses virtually no insect- or decay-resisting properties, so in general cannot be used for any kind of outdoor construction work.

Nordmann fir is propagated in nature wholly through seed dispersal, although cuttings will also take in summer and early autumn. Individual male and female flowers form high up in the tree, and the females, when fertilized, mature into erect cones. These can be up to 20 centimetres (8 in) long, containing as many as 200 scaly bracts; each bract bears a pair of winged seeds that are released as the bract distintegrates and falls off, not as part of a complete cone, but individually, leaving a central 'core' on the tree.

NORDMANN FIR

Evergreen

NATIVE TO *Eastern Europe*
HEIGHT *85 m (279 ft)*
TRUNK DIAMETER *2 m (7 ft)*
TRUNK GIRTH *6.25 m (21 ft)*
SPREAD *5 m (16 ft)*

ABOVE *Nordmann fir are popular Christmas trees, as they tend not to shed their needles.*

LEFT *Young shoots of Nordmann fir bear needles with white bands on either side of a green midrib.*

NOBLE FIR

Abies procera

Justifiably called a 'noble' fir, this is a veritable giant of a tree, occasionally rising 90 metres (295 ft) into the clouds. Laid on the ground, such a specimen would fall just short of the length of an international soccer pitch. It is a native of both the Cascade and Northern Coast mountain ranges that march close to the Pacific seaboard of the United States, where it thrives at high altitudes of up to 1,500 metres (4,921 ft).

The species was first discovered in an Oregon river valley in 1827 by the much-acclaimed botanist David Douglas, and it is the largest of the true firs in terms of height, girth and volume of timber contained in its mighty trunk. With its range extending from Washington to northern California, the biggest specimens of noble fir are to be found among those standing in the Mount St Helens National Volcanic Monument. Living on mountainsides regularly swept by storm-force winds, and with such lofty dimensions, the tree has needed to develop a high degree of mechanical flexibility, and its ability to sway dramatically allows it to cope with inclement conditions. It is also a pioneer tree that can quickly recolonize disturbed or fire-damaged ground. It does, however, require an equable climate with cool summers and mild, damp winters and prefers life on gentle slopes facing south.

Noble fir grows with a narrowly conical profile, a rounded top and short, nearly horizonal branches until it is well into its maturity. The outline tends to become more ragged after the first 200 years of growth, but even at this age it is still a young tree, since a specimen Noble fir can occasionally survive in the wild for 600 years. The trunk is clothed in a thin, smooth grey bark marked only with resin blisters, but the bark becomes more thickened, reddish and deeply fissured in old trees. The short, flattened needles are blue-green in colour and are arranged in spirals on the stems. They are also curved at the base like little twisted hockey sticks so that they tend to sweep upwards.

The male cones are rounded and crowded along the undersides of the shoots, turning bright crimson before they release their pollen, borne on the wind to the female cones. These generally appear on the same tree, and are upright and cylindrical. Carried near the crown of the tree they are at first pale yellow-green, clothed with bracts that almost cover the cone scales. The scales turn brown as they ripen and then fall away to release the little winged seeds.

These days the tree is grown extensively as an ornamental, and has also become popular as a Christmas tree.

NOBLE FIR

Evergreen

NATIVE TO *Western North America*
HEIGHT *90 m (295 ft)*
TRUNK DIAMETER *2.7 m (9 ft)*
TRUNK GIRTH *8 m (26 ft)*
SPREAD *5 m (16 ft)*

ABOVE *A young cone, fat, upright and with a dense covering of bracts.*

LEFT *A troop of the bare, grey trunks of noble fir marches silently into the distant gloom of a northern conifer forest.*

WHISTLING THORN

Acacia drepanolobium

The whistling thorn is perhaps one of the oddest trees in this collection, but it also has its place in the familiar landscape of the open African savannah. One of a number of thorny *Acacia* species found in such arid locations, it is also a party to a bizarre, mutually-beneficial living arrangement that has developed between the tree and its insect tenants – in this case, several species of tiny stinging ant.

Threats to trees come in various guises, but on the open African plains one of the more serious dangers arises from the presence of elephants and other large browsing animals for which anything green represents food. The whistling thorn is equipped with formidable spines up to 7 centimetres (3 in) long that, in theory, should counter such attacks. However, a giraffe will simply wrap its long, prehensile tongue around the foliage, avoiding the spines, and an elephant will take the easy option of knocking down the entire tree. So an additional defence is required, and it comes in the shape of four different species of stinging ant that colonize the hollow, bulbous bases of the spines and provide a remarkably effective defensive army, deterring even elephants.

Whistling thorn is native to east Africa. A comparatively small tree, it grows to little more than 6 metres (20 ft) in height and produces a pair of thorns at each point where leaves arise. Some of these become modified, two or three becoming joined at their bases by bulbous swellings about 2 centimetres (1 in) in diameter. The 'whistling' noise is created when the wind blows through the small holes made by the ants as entry and exit 'doors' in the hollow thorn bases. If any untoward movement occurs, the ants swarm out and attack the intruder, while in return the tree provides its lodgers with sugary secretions on which they feed.

The foliage, in common with that of other *Acacia* species, consists of leaves whose surface area is reduced to small pinnae or leaflets in order to combat water loss, and which are also shed during the dry season. At the onset of the brief rainy period of the year, the tree erupts with creamy white blossoms before the new season's leaves appear, and these take the form of small pom-poms not unlike those seen in mimosa. After fertilization, the ripe fruit develops as a long seed pod.

This is not the only species of *Acacia* to rely on ants for protection. The bullhorn acacia, *Acacia cornigera*, whose native range is Mexico and Central America, develops hollowed-out thorns that look rather like miniature cattle horns, and these too become occupied by colonies of aggressively stinging ants.

WHISTLING THORN

Deciduous (briefly)

NATIVE TO *African savannahs*
HEIGHT *6 m (20 ft)*
TRUNK DIAMETER *0.4 m (1 ft)*
TRUNK GIRTH *1.25 m (4 ft)*
SPREAD *7.5 m (25 ft)*

ABOVE *The inflated base of each thorn provides a refuge for ants whose tiny entrance doorways whistle when the wind blows.*

LEFT *The stark, flat-topped silhouette of this inhabitant of the open African savannahs can give welcome relief from the midday heat.*

SNAKE BARK MAPLE
Acer davidii

If credit is to be given for its introduction to the West, this eye-catching tree originating from China should more properly be called Père David's maple. In about 1862, the Basque-born missionary Armand David was the first to record it growing in the uplands of central China. But its existence was forgotten until English botanist Charles Maries came upon it during a visit to Jiangsu in 1878. Commissioned by the plant nurserymen James Veitch and Sons of Chelsea, Maries was seeking out new and hardy exotics to grace English gardens at home.

In reality snake bark maple is not a single species, since there are some 20 species of the tree worldwide, of which Père David's is the best known. The different forms when cultivated, however, are often confused in their labelling. With a single exception found in North America, all originate from southeastern Asia, growing in mixed forests up to altitudes of 1,600 metres (5,249 ft), and they are distinguished from other maples by the extrordinary patterning of their bark. Père David's maple grows in the wild more or less all the way down the China Sea coast, and in central and western China in the hilly provinces of Gansu and Yunnan.

A pretty tree, with spreading, slightly arching branches, Père David's maple grows to a maximum height of 15 metres (49 ft), generally smaller, with a more or less equal spread, and it quite often develops with more than one trunk. The branches bear serrated, broadly oval, or sometimes three-lobed, glossy, dark green leaves with bright red stalks, and the leaves turn gradually to vibrant shades of yellow, gold and red as the autumn season advances. It is, however, the dramatic patterning of the bark that captures most of the attention. Although smooth and purple-red on the youngest shoots, it changes to olive-green after the first season and then quickly develops the pale, narrow, vertical stripes that give the trunk its snake-like pattern. Two subspecies are recognized, Père David's maple and Hers' maple, each of which differs slightly in the colour of its stripes and leaf stalks.

The little decorative pendants of sweet-scented, green-yellow flowers develop in early summer as racemes, or flower clusters, and the fruits that follow, winged 'keys' or samaras, turn slowly from green to rich red, matching the foliage.

SNAKE BARK MAPLE

Deciduous

NATIVE TO *Central China*
HEIGHT *15 m (49 ft)*
TRUNK DIAMETER *0.5 m (2 ft)*
TRUNK GIRTH *1.6 m (5 ft)*
SPREAD *15 m (49 ft)*

ABOVE *Rich foliage colours provide a further eye-catching feature as winter approaches.*

LEFT *The remarkable stripy decoration of the trunk and branches make the snake bark maple a popular ornamental tree in gardens.*

SYCAMORE

Acer pseudoplatanus

Of all the tree species to be found in woodlands, parklands and urban streets, sycamore has to be ranked one of the most common. A fairly large deciduous tree with a broadly domed profile, it is fast growing and is remarkably tolerant of pollution from both vehicle emissions and salt spray. For these reasons, it is popular with urban authorities for planting along roadside verges.

Also sometimes referred to as 'sycamore maple', both the Latin and common names of this tree are revealing in different respects. *Pseudoplatanus* is an indication that it is actually not related to the *Platanus* or plane tree genus, which also thrives in urban environments, although in Scotland it is more commonly known as a plane tree. Nor is it related to the Biblical tree species called 'sycamore', since this is more correctly a species of fig, *Ficus sycomorus*, and the only similarity between the two is in the shape of the leaves.

Native to mountainous areas of central Europe and southwest Asia, *Acer pseudoplatanus* is an opportunist tree that will quickly colonize any bare or waste ground, other than in very poor soils, and it is now found in woodlands all over Europe and the British Isles. The species is also found in parts of North America, most notably New England, as an escape from cultivation. With its large leaves and tolerant character, it is often used as a windbreak on the edges of plantations, and in bygone times it was regularly planted around farmyards to provide shade from the summer heat for cattle and dairymaids alike. The earliest historical record of such a tree, grown in England, is from 1578. Sycamores are tough and resilient and individually can achieve robust old age. The so-called Tolpuddle Tree, named in honour of the Tolpuddle Martyrs in Dorset, is reckoned to have first taken root over 320 years ago.

Sycamore grows rapidly to a height of 30 metres (98 ft) or more and develops a broad leafy crown borne up on a stout, grey trunk that appears smooth in young trees but becomes scaly and roughened with age. The dark green foliage that opens in spring consists of broadly palmate, oppositely arranged leaves with toothed margins. Flowers are yellow-green and monoecious, so they include both male and female parts. The inflorescence emerges inconspicuously in spring in the form of pendulous racemes with up to 50 flowers on a stalk, and pollination is by insects, most frequently bees. The fruits that result from fertilization develop as twin samaras, each consisting of a seed with a large wing attached that allows it to rotate like a little propeller when it falls and thus disperse more effectively in the autumn winds.

SYCAMORE

Deciduous

NATIVE TO *Central Europe, North America, southwest Asia*
HEIGHT *30 m (98 ft)*
TRUNK DIAMETER *1.5 m (5 ft)*
TRUNK GIRTH *4.7 m (15 ft)*
SPREAD *22 m (72 ft)*

ABOVE *Inconspicuous yellow-green flowers erupt in little pendulous racemes in early springtime.*

LEFT *A lone mature sycamore, preparing for the onset of winter, is framed by a majestic backdrop of mountains in the Austrian Tyrol.*

CANADIAN RED MAPLE

Acer rubrum

If a single deciduous tree species epitomizes our romantic ideals of North American wilderness, it is surely the red maple. Since February 1965 its leaf has formed the centrepiece of the Canadian national flag, and as a commonly encountered tree throughout the New England region it has also become recognized as the state emblem of Rhode Island. Its foliage brings a joyous brushwork of colour to vast swathes of autumn forest throughout eastern North America.

The red maple is undoubtedly one of the most beautiful of the world's deciduous trees and in Canada especially it has left its mark on historical and cultural development. Its twigs, seeds and flowers all take on a striking red hue in contrast to the pale grey of the mature bark – but above all it is the brilliant, deep scarlet of the autumnal leaves that forms the tree's crowning glory. Sadly, of 129 species of maple known worldwide, 54 are under serious threat of extinction in their native habitats. One of the principal culprits is the Asian longhorned beetle, *Anoplophora glabripennis*, accidently introduced to North America, whose larvae with their voracious appetite for maple wood have destroyed tens of thousands of trees in Canada and the eastern United States. If unaffected by such invasion or other diseases, it reaches maturity in about 70 years but rarely lives for longer than 150, and so has a comparatively short lifespan.

A medium to large tree that can occasionally exceed 30 metres (98 ft) in height, it generally grows into a fairly rounded profile with a spread of up to a 22 metres (72 ft), and its upper branches characteristically arch outwards. The leaves, as in most maple species, are palmate, separated into between three and five lobes, and each is distinctly veined. In common with all maples, the leaves are arranged in opposite pairs along the branch. As autumn approaches, chemical changes in the leaves remove the green chlorophyll pigment and expose the striking red hues that make the tree such a delight to the eye.

In early spring the branches bear pendulous racemes of bright, cherry-red flowers, generally with males and females in separate clusters. Although individually they are small, collectively the flowers borne on the tips of the young branches also make a captivating display, each with five tiny petals enclosing a bunch of about ten long-stalked stamens, tipped with crimson. In autumn the winged fruits or 'keys', botanically known as double samaras, are cleverly designed to spin like little propellers when they fall, thus catching the wind and often being carried for considerable distances.

CANADIAN RED MAPLE

Deciduous

NATIVE TO *North America*
HEIGHT *30 m (98 ft)*
TRUNK DIAMETER *0.6 m (2 ft)*
TRUNK GIRTH *1.8 m (6 ft)*
SPREAD *22 m (72 ft)*

ABOVE *The foliage of many maples takes on a characteristic lobed, palmate apperarance, like fluttering leafy hands.*

LEFT *October foliage of the red maple paints a riot of fiery reds and golds across much of the woodland fastnesses of North America.*

MALAGASY BAOBAB
Adansonia madagascariensis

The Australian writer Ernestine Hill has given us a scintillating description of the baobab trees growing in her own country: 'A Caliban of a tree, a grizzled, distorted old goblin with the girth of a giant, the hide of a rhinoceros, twiggy fingers clutching at empty air, and the disposition of a guardian angel.' However, the location of most of the world's baobabs is in regions of Africa, and if a single living form epitomizes our romantic and exotic thoughts of the continent south of the Sahara, it is surely the bizarre silhouette of the 'upside-down tree'.

The true Malagasy baobab is one of six species endemic to Madagascar in the Indian Ocean. All baobabs originate from Africa but it is believed that in the distant past some their fruits were transported on ocean currents to take root as far away as Australia. The chief characteristics that make baobabs in general so distinctive in the landscape are their massive trunks and comparatively small, compact crowns, and this species is no exception. Although not the biggest of the bunch, it can grow to a height of 20 metres (66 ft). Its trunk is usually smooth and bottle shaped, but can also be tapering or cylindrical. Being deciduous, the branches are regularly leafless for long periods, contributing to the distorted appearance suggesting that the roots are spreading out from the top of the trunk and giving it the popular name of 'upside-down tree'.

The tree grows in both the dry and moist deciduous forests situated on the western side of the island. Alas, its populations have been extensively depleted in the last hundred years or so, a consequence of slash-and-burn farming, and its conservation status is now said to be in urgent need of review.

Because the trees have been required to evolve a survival technique through dry seasons that often last for many months, the baobabs will happily shed their leaves for the duration, thus dramatically cutting down on transpiration; the wood is also very soft and fibrous, allowing it to store considerable reserves of water. The large, pendulous fruits are an important local source of vitamin C, containing up to ten times the vitamin content of oranges. Fibre known as bast is extracted from the inner bark to be used in rope making, a practice common among the indigenous populations in Madagascar on account of the medicinal properties of the bark. The bark itself has a remarkable capacity for regeneration, even when the bark has in places been removed around the entire circumference of the trunk, a process called girdling or ring-barking.

MALAGASY BAOBAB

Deciduous (briefly)

NATIVE TO *Madagascar*
HEIGHT *20 m (66 ft)*
TRUNK DIAMETER *3.8 m (12 ft)*
TRUNK GIRTH *12 m (39 ft)*
SPREAD *12 m (39 ft)*

ABOVE *The pendulous fruit of the baobab contains large amounts of vitamin C.*

LEFT *This parade of 'upside-down trees' lines the famous Avenue des Baobabs, in Menabe, Madagascar.*

YELLOW BUCKEYE

Aesculus flava

The name *Aesculus* was first coined for these trees by the 18th-century Swedish biologist, Carl Linnaeus, who borrowed the Latin for an edible acorn, and it is known that the seeds of some of the species after leaching were eaten in Japan up until about 300 CE. Throughout North America the trees are known as buckeyes, while in Europe and Asia they are generally referred to as horse chestnuts.

An attractive-looking, hardy deciduous tree that can attain a height of 30 metres (98 ft) or more, borne up on a straight trunk with gracefully drooping branches creating a broad, rounded outline, yellow buckeye is one of 19 similar species found in the northern hemisphere. It is the largest of the North American-related species and grows principally in the Great Smoky Mountains of North Carolina and Tennessee, although it is found extensively right across the southeastern quarter of the United States. Although generally these trees reach only a moderate height, the largest living specimen in the United States stands at over 45 metres (148 ft) tall. Preferring life in river valleys, yellow buckeyes are best known for their large, showy, insect-pollinated flowers that bloom in late spring, and for the shiny ripe seeds or 'conkers' much favoured by children as autumn gets underway. Creating an oval or slightly spreading canopy with large, dark green leaves, it makes an excellent shade tree.

The bark is smooth or slightly furrowed and grey in young trees, but later develops with large scaly plates or patches. The leaves, unfolding from fat, sticky buds coated with protective resin, are sharply serrated and arranged on the branch in opposite pairs. Each is dark green and deeply divided into five or occasionally seven broad, oval-pointed leaflets. In autumn, uncommonly among horse chestnuts, the foliage turns a rich shade of orange-yellow for a few weeks, making the tree a pretty ornamental in parks and gardens.

Yellow buckeye gets its name partly from the flowers, which are solitary, creamy yellow marked with red and arise as prominent upright clusters or 'panicles' as much as 20 centimetres (8 in) tall. The 'buckeye' in the name comes from the appearance of the nut, which is encased in a leathery capsule until ripe. The capsule then splits into two valves and generally delivers two shiny brown nuts, each with a distinctive white 'buckeye'.

The timber of yellow buckeye is among the softest of hardwoods, and so its commercial use is largely limited to pulp making.

YELLOW BUCKEYE

Deciduous

NATIVE TO *North America*
HEIGHT *30 m (98 ft)*
TRUNK DIAMETER *0.6 m (2 ft)*
TRUNK GIRTH *1.8 m (6 ft)*
SPREAD *22 m (72 ft)*

ABOVE *The flowers that emerge in prominent upright yellow clusters give the tree part of its common name. 'Buckeye' refers to the distinctive decoration of the fruit.*

LEFT *A close relative of the European horse chestnut, yellow buckeye is the largest of the native* Aesculus *found in North America.*

HORSE CHESTNUT

Aesculus hippocastanum

As any child will advise you, the horse chestnut is the big, spreading tree equipped with conkers. However, the origin of its curious common name is less familiar. Although coming from an entirely different genus of trees, the fruits look not unlike the edible 'chestnuts' of *Castanea* species, and in bygone times they allegedly cured horses of chest complaints when the animals ate them: a fallacy, because the fruits are poisonous to all but a few animals.

A large species by any standards, a mature horse chestnut can achieve a height of 36 metres (118 ft), with a massive rounded canopy of stout branches that characteristically turn upwards at their outer ends. The peculiarly European association with horses is strengthened on account of the horseshoe-shaped 'saddle scar' left on the twig after each leaf has fallen, although in North America the horse association is lost and *Aesculus* species are called 'buckeyes' because of the round, pale scar on the nut.

Native to mountainous regions of eastern Europe and western Asia, though at greatest concentration in the Balkans, the horse chestnut is a fast-growing deciduous tree that will tolerate a wide range of moderate or cool climatic conditions. In spring the branch tips are clothed with fat, sticky brown buds that unfold into generous palmate leaves divided typically into seven leaflets, and in April and May the tips of the branches erupt with clusters or panicles of candle-like blossoms. Creamy white, each decorated with a little red spot, and including both male and female parts, these splendid blooms reach 20 centimetres (8 in) in height. A popular hybrid is now grown that produces pink-red flowers. The glossy red-brown nuts that mature in autumn, ready to fall from their knobbly green outer shells into the waiting grasp of children, are much sought after for a game of conkers.

Although its timber is of very little commercial value, being soft and weak, these days the horse chestnut is much favoured worldwide for planting as an ornamental in avenues, parks, ornamental gardens, and notably in Bavarian beer gardens where it creates extensive shade. One of the more well-known European examples was a majestic specimen of about 170 years of age that stood in the centre of Amsterdam until it was demolished in a storm during August 2010. This was the 'Anne Frankboom' visible from the annexe where Anne Frank and her family hid from the Nazis, and which she described in her *Diary of a Young Girl* (first published in 1947).

HORSE CHESTNUT

Deciduous

NATIVE TO *Eastern Europe, western Asia*
HEIGHT *36 m (118 ft)*
TRUNK DIAMETER *0.7 m (2 ft)*
TRUNK GIRTH *2 m (7 ft)*
SPREAD *30 m (98 ft)*

ABOVE *The spiny green casing of the horse chestnut fruit holds one or more red-brown nuts that are liberated when it falls and hits the ground.*

LEFT *A blaze of white 'candles' lights up horse chestnuts during spring.*

PERSIAN SILK TREE

Albizia julibrissin

The leaves of this tree have the curious habit of slowly closing at dusk and in rain, with the leaflets drooping downwards as if nodding off. This has led to the popular modern name of the 'night sleeper' or 'sleeping tree' in several parts of the world, including the Middle East and Japan. The Latin name of the plant is in honour of the Florentine nobleman Filippo degli Albizzi, who first introduced the Persian silk tree to Europe in the mid-18th century from its native ranges in southwestern and eastern Asia.

Also known as pink siris and sometimes incorrectly named 'mimosa' in the United States, this pretty, deciduous tree belongs to the pea or legume family. It is either much loved by horticulturalists and widely planted as an ornamental for its delicate, scented flowers, or equally loathed as a pest because of its invasive abilities once it escapes. Smallish in stature but growing rapidly to about 12 metres (39 ft), the tree can spread widthways to at least twice its height with a flat crown of arching branches. It thus creates attractive areas of dappled shade in parks and gardens, but at the same time it can form dense stands along woodland margins and in scrubland, readily ousting native plants by depriving them of sunlight and nutrients. Like many opportunistic weeds, the Persian silk tree produces seeds with strongly resistant coats that can lie dormant in the soil for many years, ready to germinate in any disturbed ground, and the trees themselves will also quickly regenerate if cut down. Research currently under way in the USA is looking to produce cultivars that will not set seed and can therefore be planted with less risk.

Generally the Persian silk tree is short lived, because it is vulnerable to a fungal parasite that causes a vascular wilting disease, although one huge and veteran example of a related species, *Albizia saman*, has survived for several hundred years as the 'Samàn del Guère', near the 'garden city' of Maracay in north-central Venezuela.

The trees, with smooth, light brown bark, are clothed with fern-like, finely divided leaves, described botanically as being pinnately compound, each about 20 centimetres (8 in) long and borne alternately along the stems. The small flowers are grouped in bunches of two or three, each decorated with tiny petals and long, dense, showy clusters of delicate pastel pink stamens, from which it earns the name pink siris. The flowers of modern cultivars can also be white, cream, pale yellow or red-tipped. Seeds are borne in flat, brown 'pea pods' and can be produced by the tree in large quantities.

PERSIAN SILK TREE

Deciduous

NATIVE TO *Eastern Asia*
HEIGHT *12 m (39 ft)*
TRUNK DIAMETER *0.6 m (2 ft)*
TRUNK GIRTH *1.8 m (6 ft)*
SPREAD *24 m (79 ft)*

ABOVE *The dense clusters of stamens create a pretty display on this popular garden tree.*

LEFT *Though unrelated to the true* Mimosa *genus, the leaves of the Persian silk tree mimic those of mimosa by drooping and folding together at night as if falling asleep.*

COMMON ALDER

Alnus glutinosa

From about 16,000 years ago, when the Earth warmed and the last glaciation started its retreat, the alder was among the first trees to colonize areas of Europe left barren by the ice, spreading north from refuges in the Balkans, Spain and Turkey by as much as 2,000 metres (6,562 ft) a year. Today the alder, its seeds spread mainly by water, occurs across Europe as far as the Caucasus, frequently growing along the banks of rivers.

A deciduous tree, also known as the European alder and black alder, it is best suited to life in wetlands with a high water table, allowing it to keep its roots in water. The specialized ecological conditions in which the alder generally thrives are known as 'carrs'. Although predominantly consisting of alder, these support other woodland trees and shrubs, including willow and hazel, all growing well on boggy or marshy soils in low-lying situations with high peat content. Having predominantly been a European tree, the common alder has also now become naturalized in parts of eastern North America.

An alder roots deeply, thus helping to limit the effects of river erosion. The presence of the tree in wetlands also markedly improves soil fertility, because its roots form a symbiotic relationship with a nitrogen-fixing bacterium that absorbs nitrogen from the atmosphere into nodules on the tree's roots and fixes the gas in a form available to the tree as food. This soil-enriching ability makes the alder an important pioneer species in ecological succession.

Mature trees are conical in profile, clad with rounded, toothed leaves, which when young are coated with a slightly sticky resin, leading to the Latin name *glutinosa*. From a distance the shape of an alder sometimes resembles a conifer, and individuals can reach a height of 35 metres (115 ft). In earlier times alder carrs were frequently coppiced for their timber which, although quite soft, is virtually waterproof and makes an ideal building material for underwater structures such as jetties and bridge supports. Among these are the pilings of the famous Rialto Bridge in Venice. White when first cut, the timber rapidly turns a pale red colour; past uses included clog making and the manufacture of charcoal for gunpowder.

The flowers of alder are catkins, pollinated by wind in the early spring before the leaves open. The male catkins are pendulous, similar to those of birch and hazel, but the female flowers borne on the same tree are short and squat, turning from green to dark brown in colour, hard, rather woody, and looking not unlike small pine cones. When ripe, they set free little seeds equipped with 'wings' containing air sacs that allow them to float on water. The seeds can actually germinate in water and then take root where they are washed up on land.

COMMON ALDER

Deciduous

NATIVE TO *Europe, western Asia*
HEIGHT *35 m (115 ft)*
TRUNK DIAMETER *0.5 m (2 ft)*
TRUNK GIRTH *1.6 m (5 ft)*
SPREAD *20 m (66 ft)*

ABOVE *The female catkins are designed to receive wind-blown pollen from their male counterparts before the leafy canopy opens in spring.*

LEFT *A leafless common alder decked with hoar frost overhangs the bank of a mountain stream.*

CASHEW NUT TREE

Anacardium occidentale

The name *Anacardium* provides a clue to the shape of an unusual fruit-like feature peculiar to this evergreen of the southern hemisphere, because it has the appearance of an upside-down heart. '*Cardium*' means 'heart' and '*ana*' means 'upwards'. However the prominent so-called cashew 'apple' is not a true fruit and it merely serves as a pedestal for the fruit proper, the cashew nut, which looks much like a little curly tail perched on the apple's tip.

The cashew nut tree is a comparatively small species, with a short, distorted trunk and flat-spreading top, rarely exceeding 12 metres (39 ft) in height. Native to Central America and the northern parts of South America, with the local name *cajueiro*, it has been in use by indigenous tribes since time immemorial as an all-round medicinal remedy. Its existence was first recorded by European explorers in 1578 and plants were then carried by entrepreneurial Portuguese traders to Goa in India. From India, the tree became naturalized extensively in tropical parts of Africa and other pantropical regions of southeast Asia, where it is cultivated for its nuts and apples.

The cashew bears leathery, broadly ovate green leaves that are spirally arranged on the branches. The small, pale green-yellow flowers, equipped with five slender petals, are carried in panicles at the branch tips and become pink as they open during the dry season. The branches spread low and winding close to the ground, and tend to take root where they touch the soil.

The cashew apple, in botanical terms, is a combination of the greatly expanded pedicel, or flower stalk, and the flower receptacle, so it is technically a false fruit. Nonetheless, it is soft and juicy, refreshingly sweet and makes good eating. The true fruit on the end of the apple is a kidney-shaped drupe containing a single seed, the familiar cashew nut, surrounded by a hard double shell that is poisonous, causing skin allergy to the extent that the seeds have to be washed and roasted before eating to remove the toxins. In practice, the drupe develops first and the 'apple' then swells out behind it.

As a consequence of its rooting arrangements, the overall tree can attain a remarkable span. The world's largest cashew nut tree stands at Pirangi do Norte in Brazil, and in 1994 it entered the *Guinness Book of Records*, having been calculated to cover an area of about 8,000 square metres (26,247 sq ft). Believed to have been planted in about 1888, it produces over 60,000 fruits annually.

CASHEW NUT TREE

Evergreen

NATIVE TO *Northern South America*
HEIGHT *12 m (39 ft)*
TRUNK DIAMETER *Variable*
TRUNK GIRTH *Variable*
SPREAD *30 m (98 ft) or more*

ABOVE *The dry-season flowers of the cashew nut tree are small and inconspicuous.*

LEFT *Cashew nuts are well known to most of us, but the curious false fruits from which they are collected when ripe may not be so familiar.*

SYDNEY RED GUM

Angophora costata

A massive red gum once grew in the Angophora Reserve, Sydney, established in 1937 with the intention of preserving the specimen, believed to be the oldest and largest of its kind. Not unusually tall at an estimated 35 metres (115 ft), its trunk had developed to 10 metres (33 ft) in girth and it was calculated to have already been a sturdy sapling in the mid-17th century. Its vast trunk has been left standing since it died after a prolonged drought in 1993. The largest red gum alive today stands at Hobsonville near Auckland on the North Island of New Zealand.

The Sydney red gum is not a gum tree in the true sense since it does not belong to the *Eucalyptus* genus, although it has a similar appearance. Its native range is in the eastern coastal forests of New South Wales and southern Queensland on well-drained, rocky, sandstone soils with poor nutrients. The species is also known as the smooth-barked apple or rose gum because of the salmon pink colour of its even, fresh bark, which becomes exposed after the older pale grey or sometimes rusty bark is shed in large flakes in springtime.

Generally achieving a height of 20 to 25 metres (66–82 ft), the Sydney red gum, with its spreading, gnarled limbs often contorted into grotesque shapes, stands as a striking figure in the Australian landscape although it can also grow in quite stunted forms with multiple stems, known as mallee. The wood is brittle, making the branches prone to snap easily, and where they have shattered their stumps form rounded, callous-like lumps on the trunk, thus creating an even more distorted appearance.

The leaves, slenderly lance shaped, are carried in dark green, opposite rows along the branches, which distinguishes them from those of true eucalyptus species where the leaves are borne in alternate rows. The leaf buds are also distinct from those of eucalyptus, with little pointed ribs but without a bud cap.

Flowering in December and January, at the height of the antipodean summer, the blossoms, with five large semi-circular petals and long stamens, are borne at the tips of the branches in panicles, creamy white and showy. But it is the fruit capsules, which develop after the flowers, that provide the tree with its Latin name. The genus name *Angophora* comes from the Greek word for a goblet, and the species name refers to the five lengthwise ribs ending in teeth on the surface of the capsule, since 'costate' means ribbed.

SYDNEY RED GUM

Evergreen

NATIVE TO *Eastern Australia*
HEIGHT *25 m (82 ft)*
TRUNK DIAMETER *1.5 m (5 ft)*
TRUNK GIRTH *4.7 m (15 ft)*
SPREAD *20 m (66 ft)*

ABOVE *Though not a member of the* Eucalyptus *genus of true gum trees, this species similarly exudes a sticky resin from its trunk.*

LEFT *The rays of the setting sun bring out the warm colours of the smooth, rosy-hued bark on account of which the tree is aptly named.*

MONKEY PUZZLE TREE

Araucaria araucana

One of the great iconic trees but also among the most ancient, this is in many respects a living fossil, which can live for as long as 1,000 years. Also called the Chilean pine, fossilized remains from the Jurassic period indicate that its ancestry spans a vast period. It populated the Earth in the age of the great reptiles such as the dinosaurs 150 million years ago. Discovered in about 1780 by a Spanish explorer, its native range is now chiefly restricted to the lower slopes of the Chilean and Argentinian Andes.

Brought from Chile by a naval surgeon, Archibald Menzies, in 1795, its edible seeds were allegedly served as a dessert during a dinner with the Chilean governor. Menzies sowed a few of the seeds in a frame on the quarter deck of the ship in which he sailed back to Europe, and one of saplings that germinated was then planted in Kew Gardens, London, where it stood until 1892. Monkey puzzle is now grown as a hardy ornamental in various temperate parts of the world. Nonetheless, it is increasingly threatened with extinction in its natural habitat, and its trade or export is only permitted under exceptional circumstances. During much of the 19th century, the trees were extensively felled and logged by Europeans who exploited the timber for pit props, railway sleepers, and even for the masts of sailing ships. Today the biggest threat to survival from the human population is mainly that of fire resulting from agricultural clearance, and in 1971 the tree became protected by law, making it an offence to cut it down or cause it damage in its protected areas. In 1990, it was declared a Chilean National Monument.

A cone-bearing evergreen, growing to a magnificent 40 metres (131 ft) tall, it displays a top-heavy triangular outline shaped like an umbrella, and its long slender tiers of branches are completely covered with dark green, glossy leaves. These are sharp pointed and overlapping, making the tree more or less impossible to climb and so giving it the popular name of monkey puzzle. The female cones are smooth and globular, up to 20 centimetres (8 in) in diameter, each holding some 200 seeds that are released when the cone disintegrates on ripening. The cones of the male are oblong and in appearance are reminiscent of cucumbers. The trees are generally single sexed and pollination is by wind action, but a tree does not normally produce seed until it is about 40 years of age, which makes planting it for commercial timber production uneconomical.

MONKEY PUZZLE TREE

Evergreen

NATIVE TO *South America*
HEIGHT *40 m (131 ft)*
TRUNK DIAMETER *2 m (7 ft)*
TRUNK GIRTH *6.25 m (21 ft)*
SPREAD *20 m (66 ft)*

ABOVE *The globular female cones of the monkey puzzle stand upright on young branches.*

LEFT *A mature monkey puzzle in the Villarrica National Park, high in the Andes mountains of Chile, framed by one of a trio of volcanoes.*

With a fresh layer of snow, these famous monkey puzzle trees in the Malalcahuello National Reserve in Chile give the area a mythical air.

PACIFIC MADRONE

Arbutus menziesii

Admired for its intriguingly misshapen limbs, attractive peeling bark, showy blossoms and brightly coloured fruits, the evergreen Pacific madrone is a species often chosen to add aesthetic beauty and colour to man-made landscapes. Yet it is also under severe threat, and currently there are concerted efforts under way to halt a downward spiral in the welfare of the madrone in its native ranges along the Pacific coast, from British Columbia to the west-facing slopes of the northern Sierra Nevada.

A comparatively small tree growing up to 30 metres (98 ft) in height, but generally much less, and belonging to the *Erica* or heather genus, its European counterparts are commonly called strawberry trees because of the superficial resemblance of the fruit to a strawberry. The Spanish word *madrono* carries a similar meaning. The species epithet 'menzies' was added in honour of the Scottish botanist Archibald Menzies, who first named the tree during a voyage of discovery along the Pacific coast with the British Navy between 1791 and 1795.

The Pacific madrone has thick, evergreen leaves, broadly oval and glossily green on their upper surface, arranged in spirals along the stems. The trunk, or sometimes multiple trunks, decorated with a rich orange-red bark that regularly strips away on the mature wood, is curved and has a heavy, spreading crown of distorted or misshapen limbs.

The blossoms that generally emerge in May are small and bell shaped (like those of heather), creamy white or pastel pink, and borne in clusters or panicles on the ends of the branches. Pollination is mainly carried out by bees that are attracted to the nectar, but also by hummingbirds. The little orange-red berries, about the size of peas, ripen in autumn.

The tree, which grows almost down to sea level in the north of its range but climbs to altitudes of 1,200 metres (3,937 ft) in California, will only stand mild winters and well-drained soils. Although drought tolerant, it also needs to be growing in areas where there is good seasonal rainfall. It is, nonetheless, under threat and its numbers in the wild are declining for reasons that are not entirely clear but are currently under intensive investigation. It appears to be sensitive to any changes in the drainage of its soil, and it can quickly fall victim to a virulent fungal pathogen, *Phytophthora ramorum*, but these factors do not fully explain the downward path in its fortunes. One suggestion is that the compacting of the soil in areas with dense human population may be having an adverse effect.

PACIFIC MADRONE

Evergreen

NATIVE TO *North America*
HEIGHT *30 m (98 ft)*
TRUNK DIAMETER *2.5 m (8 ft)*
TRUNK GIRTH *8 m (26 ft)*
SPREAD *15 m (49 ft)*

ABOVE *A characteristic of the species is that the bark regularly peels off in thin, papery strips, revealing a pale green layer beneath.*

LEFT *The sunlight brings a rich, softly orange glow to the smooth bark of the Pacific madrone as its characteristically twisted branches reach skywards on Saltspring Island, British Columbia.*

BREADFRUIT TREE

Artocarpus altilis

Perhaps best known to many of us for its role as a prized cargo of plants in the notorious saga of Captain William Bligh and the 1787 mutiny aboard his expeditionary ship, HMS *Bounty*, the breadfruit is a flowering tree of tropical regions south of the equator. It is cultivated as a major source of food throughout southeast Asia and the Pacific islands of Polynesia, with the exception of Easter Island and New Zealand, where the climate is too cold.

The *Artocarpus* species, of which there about 60 worldwide, are members of the mulberry family. Responding to a reasonable view that the breadfruit would provide an economical staple crop with which to feed the burgeoning population of slaves in the Caribbean colonies, Captain Bligh, having eventually found his way home after his enforced departure from the *Bounty*, did manage to transport live breadfruit plants to the West Indies from Tahiti on a second expedition in 1791. However, the exercise proved to have limited success because the slaves refused to eat their newly provided diet. Today, the world's largest collection of breadfruit varieties is to be found on the island of Hawaii.

With the exception of the eye-catching fruits, which are built like oversized green strawberries, breadfruit trees are of unremarkable appearance. Evergreen, the trees can grow to a maximum height of 26 metres (85 ft), often rather less, and the grey trunk carries big, spreading branches. The leaves are also large, thickened and deeply cut into broadly awl-shaped segments, although some varieties produce more or less entire leaves. The leaves are glossy and dark, marked with green-yellow veins. All parts of the tree produce latex, which has been popularly used for caulking boats.

Flowers of both sexes are borne on the same tree. Male flowers are club shaped with large numbers of minute blossoms, each bearing two anthers, and attached to a spongy central column. Their female counterparts consist of up to 2,000 very much reduced blossoms, also attached to a similar core. The flowers effectively fuse together and in doing so generate the fleshy edible part of what is technically a false fruit. As the breadfruit swells, the actual flower remnants are seen on the skin as little hexagonal discs. Breadfruits vary in size and shape according to the cultivated variety, but commonly run to about the size of a grapefruit. In larger varieties an individual fruit can, however, weigh in at as much as 6 kilograms (13 lbs). The fruit colour ranges from light green to yellow when ripe, and can be either smooth or spiny. The fruits have a high starch content, and are usually roasted or baked, after which they are said to taste like freshly baked bread.

BREADFRUIT TREE

Deciduous (briefly)

NATIVE TO *Pacific region*
HEIGHT *26 m (85 ft)*
TRUNK DIAMETER *1.5 m (5 ft)*
TRUNK GIRTH *4.7 m (15 ft)*
SPREAD *15 m (49 ft)*

ABOVE *The distinctive green fruits of the breadfruit tree hang from the branches like oversized strawberries.*

LEFT *The historical assocation of this tree with the mutiny on the* Bounty *led to its widespread cultivation in many tropical regions. Here, it flourishes on the Caribbean island of Barbados.*

SILVER BIRCH

Betula pendula

The silver birch has earned the popular traditional name of 'Lady of the Woods'; aptly so, beause its appearance, from the delicate silvery bark to the slender limbs, airy disposition and cascades of fluttery leaves, is thoroughly feminine. Nobody could accuse this tree of possessing the tough, macho image of an oak or elm. With ancient origins, its ancestors clothed large parts of Europe and America long before the last Ice Age, and it was one of the first pioneer species to recolonize the land left bare by the receding ice.

Betula pendula has a commonly encountered sister tree in northern Europe and in Scotland, *Betula pubescens*. The downy birch is very similar in appearance but possesses hairy shoots. Birches extend in their natural range throughout the European land mass and into parts of southwest Asia. In the more southerly latitudes of Europe, however, they only appear at higher altitudes. It is the national tree of Finland, and Canada is sometimes known as the 'Land of the Silver Birch', even if there the reference is to a different species, the paper bark birch.

The tree generally grows to about 25 metres (82 ft) in height. Always elegantly formed, it bears drooping, slender branches and a light, airy canopy. Other than the whippy twigs, which are black, the bark of the trunk and main boughs is predominantly silvery-white, shed in thin layers like tissue paper and containing dark grey or black triangular crevices. These marks are less apparent in the downy birch, in which the bark does not peel. Other visible differences between the two species lie in the bark colour (reddish becoming grey in downy birch); the smoothness of silver birch twigs where downy birch twigs are warty; and the edges of the leaves.

The leaves of silver birch are small and triangular in outline, with a pointy tip and a double-tooth, serrated edge, while those of downy birch have single teeth. In springtime the bare branches of both species become clothed with lambs' tail, dangly catkins whose male pollen is borne on the wind. The minute winged seeds of the crimson female catkins, each only a milligram or so in weight, ripen in late summer and are also carried on the wind.

Silver birch is generally found in association with a mycorrhizal fungus, the well-known red and white spotted fly agaric, that provides it with a reservoir of water and essential minerals when these are in short supply in the poor soils in which the tree generally thrives. It also serves as host to another fungal species, this time the parasitic *Taphrina betulina*, that stimulates the growth of dense tangles of twigs looking like birds' nests in the branches, popularly called 'witches' brooms'.

SILVER BIRCH

Deciduous

NATIVE TO *Europe*
HEIGHT *25 m (82 ft)*
TRUNK DIAMETER *0.5 m (2 ft)*
TRUNK GIRTH *1.6 m (5 ft)*
SPREAD *15 m (49 ft)*

ABOVE *The outer layers of bark on the trunk of the silver birch are shed like thin sheets of white tissue paper.*

LEFT *The delicate trunks and foliage of immature silver birches stand clustered in a northern forest, like ghostly apparitions with dark, staring eyes.*

FLAME OF THE FOREST

Butea monosperma

As its name suggests, the crowning glory of this tree, found growing throughout tropical and subtropical parts of the Indian subcontinent and southeast Asia, comes when the long racemes of blossoms erupt in great fiery, orange-pink cascades from the bare branches in April and May. The flowers form one of the most popular decorations during the spring Hindu festival of Holi.

A deciduous inhabitant of lowland regions and reaching little more than 15 metres (49 ft) in height, flame of the forest is a comparatively slow-growing tree. Although it can thrive in a variety of water-logged soils on the plains, it is also very drought resistant and possesses good salt tolerance. For this reason, it is often planted in coastal areas where fierce winds off the sea can distort and gnarl its limbs into bizarre shapes.

Flame of the forest displays an upright, generally rather distorted trunk and branches clothed in pale grey bark. The segmented or pinnate leaves are borne on silky young stems. Largely shed over the winter months, the leaves only return with the emergence of the blossoms that stand out so brilliantly against clear blue tropical skies. The showy flowers are pendulous and make for an indispensible colourful contribution to the celebration of spring. Each arises from a contrasting dark green sheath, or calyx, and the long racemes attract myriad butterflies and birds, which in turn serve as pollinating agents. Each flower consists of five petals comprising a standard petal, two wings and a prominent composite keel shaped like a beak that lends itself to another popular name, parrot tree. The seeds develop singly – hence the epithet *monosperma* in flat, grey pods covered in dense brown hairs. In past times the seeds are reputed to have been added to feed by Arab horse traders in order to keep their stock in good condition.

The timber is white in colour and holds water-resistant properties that make it a valuable commodity in the manufacture of utensils, and it is also used in the cladding of wells. The wood produces high-quality charcoal. Away from practical applications, the tree is sacred to Hindus, who believe it to be an emanation of the fire god, Agni, and items carved from the wood find a religious purpose in fire rituals. Dye extracted from the flowers is traditionally put to use in local cottage industries for dyeing silk. With the tree's considerable tolerance for life in swampy conditions, the blossoms also act as an effective natural control of insects, since the long corolla tube of each flower collects a liquid in which mosquitoes lay their eggs. This nursery proves to be toxic, and the eggs are destined never to hatch.

FLAME OF THE FOREST

Deciduous

NATIVE TO *India, southeast Asia*
HEIGHT *15 m (49 ft)*
TRUNK DIAMETER *0.4 m (1 ft)*
TRUNK GIRTH *1.25 m (4 ft)*
SPREAD *9 m (30 ft)*

ABOVE *Each bright red, pea-like flower forms part of a cluster or raceme, blooming before the leaves open at the end of winter.*

LEFT *This tropical tree, a member of the pea family and native to India, erupts in a riot of brilliant, showy flowers said to resemble the beaks of parrots.*

EUROPEAN HORNBEAM
Carpinus betulus

Hornbeam was among the first of the broad-leaved trees to colonize northern Europe as the ice receded at the end of the last glaciation, and although related most closely to another post-glaciation tree, the birch, hornbeam leaves bear strong similarity to those of beech. In demand not only as a tall, attractive parkland tree needing low maintenance, it also serves as good hedging material. The famous maze at Hampton Court in Surrey is believed originally to have been constituted of hornbeam, now replaced by holly and yew.

The most eye-catching feature of a European hornbeam is surely its silvery-grey bark, which develops a remarkable fluted and twisted appearance as the tree matures. One of some 40 species dispersed across the temperate regions of the northern hemisphere, the individual trees are comparatively small, rarely reaching 25 metres (82 ft) in height and frequently rather less. Hornbeam wood, however, is exceptionally hard, like horn, and gives rise to the first part of its common name. The 'beam' seems to be a corruption of the German word for a tree, *baum*. The popular name of its counterpart in North America is ironwood, or musclewood, and the extreme hardness of the timber coupled with the pressures it creates within the trunk are probably the main factors forcing the hornbeam's bark into such deep twists and fissures.

When young it is a somewhat narrowly triangular tree, though spreading in profile as it matures. It prefers life in partial shade conditions, so rarely stands on its own. It is generally to be found in woodlands in the company of larger trees such as oak and beech that screen out direct sunlight. It also requires life in a warm climate before it can achieve strong growth, and therefore the native range tends to be in the southerly parts of Europe, occuring at altitudes below 600 metres (1,969 ft). Old hornbeams often show evidence of traditional pollarding for their timber, and this feature is very noticeable in Epping Forest, just outside London, one of its strongest refuges in southern England where it is now a protected species.

The deciduous leaves alternate densely on the stems and look rather like those of beech, with serrated edges and prominent veins. However, they lack the soft furriness of a young beech leaf. Turning a pretty golden colour in autumn, some are always retained on the branches over the winter when hornbeam is used for hedging. The tree is wind pollinated and bears long, dangling, green catkins in spring. In autumn the fruits mature as winged samaras that hang in clusters from the branch tips.

EUROPEAN HORNBEAM

Deciduous

NATIVE TO *Europe*
HEIGHT *25 m (82 ft)*
TRUNK DIAMETER *0.6 m (2 ft)*
TRUNK GIRTH *1.8 m (6 ft)*
SPREAD *18 m (59 ft)*

ABOVE *The hornbeam leaf is similar to that of beech in appearance, with its serrated edges.*

LEFT *A massive veteran, still showing signs of pollarding that took place in times gone by, stands gnarled and resolute as winter approaches in a Transylvanian woodland.*

WATER HICKORY

Carya aquatica

Most commonly encountered in the Mississippi river valley, today this is one of the most significant trees in the wetter woodlands of the United States' Deep South, ranging from eastern Texas to Florida and north as far as Virginia. Related to the pecan, *Carya illinoinensis*, it is best known for its nuts, but as other trees in the region have been successively felled for their timber, water hickory has taken on a more important role in the battle against local erosion and flooding.

The tree grows chiefly along the banks of rivers and in forests on the floodplains where the inundations are short lived. It prefers soil that is light, sandy and well drained, since it will not cope with having its roots immersed in water for any length of time, and it will not thrive in deep shade. Members of the walnut family, the trees grow slowly and only after about 50 years will they achieve as much as 30 metres (98 ft) in height, readily being squeezed out by other more vigorous species. Hickory wood, however, is of limited value because it splits or 'shakes' too easily as it dries, and as a consequence of this probably more than any other factor, the tree has come to dominate many areas where high-grade logging of species with commercially valuable timber has reduced any significant competition, allowing it freedom to spread unchallenged.

Not a particularly imposing tree and otherwise looking remarkably similar to the pecan, it is best recognized by its nuts during the fruiting season. These are rough coated in a thin outer husk, dark brown and characteristically flattened with four acutely angled lengthwise ribs, but they are also bitter to taste, unlike the nuts of the pecan, and so are ignored by most foraging animals. The trunk is straight with slender, comparatively short and rather tangled branches, creating an oval outline and clothed with grey bark that tends to develop a rather loose, shaggy appearance. The dark green deciduous leaves are large pinnate, up to 45 centimetres (18 in) long, reminiscent of the ash tree, and consist of up to 13 narrow, pointed leaflets with finely serrated edges.

The catkin-like flowers that emerge in Aprtil and May present one of the prettiest features of the tree. Both males and females are borne on the same tree, and the male flowers hang in long, slender cascades waiting for their pollen to be dispersed by the wind to the very tiny yellow-green female flowers.

WATER HICKORY

Deciduous

NATIVE TO *North America*
HEIGHT *30 m (98 ft)*
TRUNK DIAMETER *0.75 m (2 ft)*
TRUNK GIRTH *2.3 m (8 ft)*
SPREAD *20 m (66 ft)*

ABOVE *The fruits of water hickory take the form of capsules, each with four lobes that split when ripe.*

LEFT *Standing at Morton Arboretum, the typically straight trunk of a mature water hickory, ascending to short rather tangled branches, is clothed in a loose, shaggy grey bark.*

SPANISH CHESTNUT

Castanea sativa

A fine, spreading tree, always popular for landscaping in England and many parts of Europe, the Spanish chestnut has been in cultivation, chiefly for its edible nuts, for more than 2,000 years since the time of the Roman Empire. A favourite for cooking over open fires, and a familiar sight on street vendors' braziers in autumn, the smell of roasted chestnuts is guaranteed to evoke thoughts of dark, chilly nights and Christmas fare.

Spanish chestnut, also known as sweet chestnut or *marron*, is a hardy deciduous species related to beech and oak, but bearing no relationship to the horse chesnut. To grow well it prefers a mild climate, since it originates from southern Europe and parts of north Africa; a closely related species, *Castanea dentata*, is found in North America. It is comparatively fast growing and individual trees may also achieve a great age. Many of England's stately homes and parks play host to gnarled and distorted veterans. A famous specimen still standing in Cucuruzzu on the French island of Corsica is reputed to have been planted over 1,000 years ago, thus first taking root at around the time of William the Conqueror.

Reaching a maximum height of about 35 metres (115 ft), older trees such as those in Petworth Park, Sussex, and a fine notable specimen standing near King William's Temple in Kew Gardens, London, may develop massive trunks with a girth around the base of more than 6 metres (20 ft). Although its initial rate of growth can be rapid, 20 years or more may pass before a tree yields its first fruit. Generating very hard, durable wood that is used in furniture making as well as for staves for the construction of barrels, in the past Spanish chestnut has been regularly coppiced, yielding good amounts of timber once every 20 or 30 years. Many aged specimens still show signs of this technique.

The rough and deeply fissured bark of the trunk develops a characteristic spiral and netted patterning that results from mechanical stresses brought on by the extreme hardness of the wood. Veterans can also develop substantial splits and at times grow into intriguing shapes. The leaves are larger and elongated with serrated edges, and blooming in July it bears separate male and female flowers that are pollinated mainly by bees. The nuts ripen in autumn, released from their protective spiny green cases (which deter foraging squirrels) only after the fruit falls to the ground. The tree was first spread from its native ranges by the Romans, who carried the seeds in their baggage to plant as a source of meal. The Roman legionnaires were allegedly regularly fed on chestnut porridge before going into battle.

SPANISH CHESTNUT

Deciduous

NATIVE TO *Southeast Europe, western Asia*
HEIGHT *35 m (115 ft)*
TRUNK DIAMETER *2 m (7 ft)*
TRUNK GIRTH *6.25 m (21 ft)*
SPREAD *22 m (72 ft)*

ABOVE *The edible nuts ripen in safety, protected by a bristly shell that deters foraging animals.*

LEFT *A veteran Spanish chestnut characteristically develops a massive gnarled and twisted trunk, attributable to the extreme hardness of the timber and the stresses it creates.*

ATLANTIC BLUE CEDAR

Cedrus atlantica 'Glauca'

Of all the fine trees to grace our 21st-century parklands and ornamental gardens, the Atlantic blue cedar must rank highly in its claim for the crown. Today it is one of the most frequently planted of ornamentals, although often far from its native climes on the cool slopes of the Atlas Mountains that span Algeria and Morocco in north Africa. It was not, however, until 1845 that the blue-tinged variety that we know so well as 'blue cedar' was first cultivated.

When at its full stretch, this is an imposingly large evergreen equipped with fine ascending branches and sometimes reaching a height of 40 metres (131 ft). One of the biggest specimens outside the Atlas Mountains, where the trees are regularly felled for timber, survives at Parco Sella in Piemonte, northern Italy. It can tolerate dry and hot climatic conditions better than many other conifers, although it tends not to do well in its native mountain ranges at altitudes lower than 1,400 metres (4,593 ft) or when exposed to salt spray off the sea. One of the best-known examples has to be a cedar planted by a past president of the United States on the south lawn of the White House in Washington, DC.

The difference between this and the closely related cedar of Lebanon is not always easy to tell, because the needles of both species can take on a blue tone. Each species has a rather triangular profile, with few branches developing at the crown. However, the branches of the cedar of Lebanon spread out on a level plane rather than pointing upwards. They can achieve much the same height, but since the cedar of Lebanon was introduced to Europe some 200 years earlier, examples of Atlantic blue cedar tend to be the smaller of the two in cultivation. Both can readily succumb to rot when they reach maturity, because pools of water become trapped between trunk and branches. As a result they are generally felled at around 150 years of age with safety in mind.

The needles of cedars are quite distinctive and different from all other conifers apart from larches, which are always deciduous. They are short and arise in little rosettes or whorls, with each set remaining on the tree for as long as four years before falling.

The newly emergent female cones are upright, somewhat cylindrical in shape, green when young and appear in late summer in the upper branches, maturing in the autumn of the second year. Their winged seeds are shed in the following spring.

ATLANTIC BLUE CEDAR

Evergreen

NATIVE TO *North Africa*
HEIGHT *40 m (131 ft)*
TRUNK DIAMETER *2 m (7 ft)*
TRUNK GIRTH *6.25 m (21 ft)*
SPREAD *25 m (82 ft)*

ABOVE *The delicate young needles are spread out in a glaucous rosette and are then destined to remain on the tree for three or four years.*

LEFT *This fine specimen of Atlantic blue cedar makes an impressive spectacle in a forest at Azrou in the Atlas Mountains of Morocco.*

CEDAR OF LEBANON

Cedrus libani

Surely one of the most elegant and graceful of all the world's coniferous trees, the cedar of Lebanon owes much of its fame to the Bible, in which it provided the timber for the construction of the Temple of Solomon in Jerusalem. But its cultural significance can be traced back to the more distant era of the Sumerian civilization nearly 10,000 years ago, when cedar groves were seen as the dwelling places of the gods. The resin of the tree was employed as part of the mummification process in ancient Egypt.

Cedar of Lebanon is a magnificent tree by any standards, growing to some 40 metres (131 ft) in height with an outline that is conical in younger trees. With age, however, the shape changes and the upper branches spread horizontally as flat tiers, so that the crown appears to be like an anvil or thunderhead. Its principal native range extends up the eastern Mediterranean from Lebanon through Syria to southern Turkey, but it is also encountered growing naturally in Cyprus and in the Atlas Mountains of Morocco. The tree thrives best on slopes facing the sea, with a good depth of soil, and at altitudes between 1,000 and 2,000 metres (3,281–6,562 ft) where it often forms pure forests.

In Biblical times the cedar forests covered vast tracts of land, but over the centuries it has fallen prey to massive deforestation for its valuable timber, and both in Lebanon, where it appears on the Lebanese flag as the national tree, and in Turkey, substantial replanting programmes have now been organized. From far back in history, its Biblical fame guaranteed export of Lebanese cedar as an ornamental tree, and the first record of it being planted in western Europe dates from 1638.

Cedrus libani is slow growing and the oldest surviving specimens in the wild are believed to be about 1,000 years of age. A fairly typical conifer, it bears cones (although not for at least 25 years from planting), and the needles arise in two different arrangements. Those on long shoots are spaced apart, but the foliage on short shoots is bunched in little tufts or whorls. Individual male and female red-coloured catkins are found on the same tree and pollination is effected by wind. The fertilized cones stand up straight on the branches, grow to about 10 centimetres (4 in) long and are barrel shaped, green when young and becoming brown at maturity. The cone takes two years to ripen, after which each scale opens and falls away from a central core, liberating two tiny winged seeds that are dispersed on the wind.

CEDAR OF LEBANON

Evergreen

NATIVE TO *Western Asia*
HEIGHT *40 m (131 ft)*
TRUNK DIAMETER *2.5 m (8 ft)*
TRUNK GIRTH *8 m (26 ft)*
SPREAD *35 m (115 ft)*

ABOVE *The tree reaches an impressive height at maturity, with characteristic flatly spreading boughs and dark, feathery foliage.*

LEFT *Evening sunlight, sweeping across the Qadisha Valley in the mountains of Lebanon, captures rugged patterns in the cedar of Lebanon's bark.*

LAWSON'S CYPRESS

Chamaecyparis lawsoniana

There can be few ornamental trees that have been planted more, either as windbreaks, screens or trees standing alone, than the different types of cypress; the most frequently sold in garden centres and tree nurseries generally being leylandii and Lawson's cypress. Fast growing, easy to maintain and either loved or hated by gardeners, the native range of Lawson's cypress lies in the American states of Oregon and California.

A stately evergreen conifer with a straight central trunk and short branches ending in flattened twigs that carry dense, flat sprays of leaves, Lawson's cypress can reach a height of 25 metres (82 ft) or more in its native range. It tends to grow in small groves on lower mountain slopes from sea level up to 1,500 metres (4,921 ft) near the coasts of southern Oregon and northern California. In the last century its populations have declined significantly in these areas for reasons that are not entirely clear, because it is an opportunist tree that germinates and grows fast when circumstances permit. Long lived, it does not reach full maturity for about 300 years, by which time it has grown into a tall conical or columnar outline, with more elongated and somewhat drooping branches. The bark is reddish-brown in colour, decorated with thick furrows, and the leaves are blue-green.

In the wild, the oldest known specimen trees are about 560 years of age, though first producing cones quite early on after as little as five years. The male cones are minute and red-brown, while their female counterparts are larger and rounded, green initially but ripening to brown. The cones first emerge in the spring, both sexes on the same tree, but do not mature until the following year when the pollen is transported on the wind currents. The little seeds that result from fertilization are also winged and light enough to journey on the breeze or float on water for their dispersal.

The Lawson's cypress was first discovered by a Scottish botanist, Andrew Murray, near Port Orford in Oregon in the mid-19th century, and was named after the horticulturalist firm of Lawson and Son, Edinburgh, where it was first grown in cultivation. The tree has very little economic value other than as an ornamental, and in this respect numerous cultivars have now been created. In terms of practical use, one notable exception is found in Japan where its timber is in demand for making high-quality coffins; it also found favour in bygone times for manufacturing arrow shafts on account of the straightness of the wood grain.

LAWSON'S CYPRESS

Evergreen

NATIVE TO *North America*
HEIGHT *25 m (82 ft)*
TRUNK DIAMETER *2 m (7 ft)*
TRUNK GIRTH *6.25 m (21 ft)*
SPREAD *5 m (16 ft)*

ABOVE *Maturing trees grown in a forest plantation display their familiar neat cone-shaped profiles, either loved or loathed by gardeners.*

LEFT *Young, still-green female cones of Lawson's cypress hang from the newest branches and display intricate patterns and shapes on surfaces where the scales are still tightly shut.*

COCONUT PALM

Cocos nucifera

A true icon of the tropics, the first known accurate description of the coconut palm is by Cosmos of Alexandria, written in about 545 CE, and according to the Arabic tale in *One Thousand and One Nights*, probably in circulation at about the same time, Sinbad the Sailor traded coconuts during one of his epic voyages. The Portuguese were effectively the first Europeans to come across the fruit in India; they named it 'coconut' from the verb *cocar*, which means to grin and refers to the three small indents in the shell resembling eyes and a nose.

These days the coconut palm, reaching about 30 metres (98 ft) in height, grows commonly right around the tropical and subtropical regions of the world and is best known for its fruit. Where it originated from in antiquity, however, remains an unresolved mystery. A very ancient plant in geological terms, traces of the ancestors of the modern coconut have been found in fossil beds of the Eocene epoch dating from between 54 and 36 million years ago, in both Australia and India. In South America, similar fossils have been discovered from even further back in time.

The coconut palm was probably spread far and wide partly because of the natural buoyant ability of its fruit to float on water, but also through human transportation since the nuts have long respresented a portable source of food and water on ocean voyages. Not a true nut but a drupe, the fleshy 'meat' contained inside its hard shell, coupled with a refreshing watery juice, is a staple part of the diet of many people throughout the tropics. The tree requires a warm climate with abundant rainfall but thrives on poor, sandy soils and tolerates a high level of salt, so it readily germinates and takes root on any suitable shore, wherever it lands up.

The coconut palm bears very long pinnate leaves in dense tufts at the top of its single, unbranched trunk, where each leaf can be as much as 6 metres (20 ft) in overall length. When old leaves fall away, they leave no scar on the bark. Flowers are tiny, yellowish-green and borne collectively in inflorescences that emerge from the leaf axils, with the male flowers arranged at the tip and the rather larger females further down towards the base. When fertilized, these transform into the massive familiar fruits up to 30 centimetres (12 in) long, each equipped with a thick, fibrous outer husk surrounding a tough, woody shell.

COCONUT PALM

Deciduous (briefly)

NATIVE TO *Indo-Pacific region*
HEIGHT *30 m (98 ft)*
TRUNK DIAMETER *0.4 m (1 ft)*
TRUNK GIRTH *1.25 m (4 ft)*
SPREAD *12 m (39 ft)*

ABOVE *Coconut fruits are designed to float on water and are thus carried on ocean currents, ready to germinate on any convenient shoreline.*

LEFT *A mature coconut palm is starkly defined against a blue tropical sky, its developing fruits visible far above in the crown among the long, feathery leaves.*

SOUTHERN CABBAGE TREE

Cordyline australis

With its palm-like leaves and decidedly exotic appearance, *Cordyline australis* is now a must-have for many European and North American parks and gardens that are far removed from its native climes in the western Pacific. Cold winters occasionally take a heavy toll on numbers because the plant is not frost-hardy, but new individuals have a remarkable ability to regenerate from the base of the old, dead trunk.

Gaining the popular name 'cabbage tree' on account of the massive, dense panicles of creamy white flowers that erupt in early summer, in other respects this tree bears scant similarity to a cabbage plant and rather more to a palm tree. The early ancestor of the cordylines arrived in Australasia from the north about 15 million years ago in the Miocene era, and it has now evolved into many different varieties. The tree first came to the enthusiastic notice of European horticulturalists when it was brought back to England in 1769 by the naturalist Joseph Banks, and it has since become popular as an ornamental in many parts of the northern hemisphere that benefit from milder climates close to the sea.

In its native ranges it grows as a lowland species up to about 1,000 metres (3,281 ft). Historical accounts from New Zealand suggest that it once formed dense jungles in swamps and along river banks. It requires plenty of light and prefers not to be over-shadowed by other vegetation. Unrestricted it can grow up to 20 metres (66 ft) in height, with a robust, straight trunk giving rise to short branches after its first flowering. The base of the trunk arises from fat, club-like underground rhizomes that serve to anchor it firmly in the soil. From the tips of the branches sprout dense clusters of narrowly sword-shaped, parallel-veined leaves, each of which can extend up to 1 metre (39 in) in length. The older bark is grey, fibrous and soft to the touch. It also bears longitudinal fissures and carries the scars of the old leaves, which bend downwards before they eventually fall away.

The flower heads are arranged as hugely eye-catching and fragrant spikes or panicles up to 100 centimetres (39 in) long. The individual flowers are comparatively tiny and are insect-pollinated, and the resulting fruit is a white berry that attracts birds as a valuable source of food. After each flowering the branch on which the inflorescence developed can then fork again, thus eventually creating the impression from a distance of a dense, rounded head on a long pole.

SOUTHERN CABBAGE TREE

Deciduous (briefly)

NATIVE TO *Western Pacific region*
HEIGHT *20 m (66 ft)*
TRUNK DIAMETER *2.5 m (8 ft)*
TRUNK GIRTH *8 m (26 ft)*
SPREAD *12 m (39 ft)*

ABOVE *The young flower buds are poised to develop into the arresting heads of creamy white flowers that give the tree its name.*

LEFT *Framed here by a New Zealand mountain backdrop, the southern cabbage tree is a lowland species believed to have once formed dense jungles along river banks.*

KOUSA DOGWOOD

Cornus kousa var. *chinensis*

Of the various species of flowering dogwood worldwide, this must surely be among the prettiest, and it has justifiably earned the Award of Garden Merit from the Royal Horticultural Society in London. With its masses of showy white flower heads and autumnal fruits looking much like strawberries, it has pride of place in the National Cornus Collection held by the RHS at its Rosemoor gardens in north Devon.

Dogwoods in general are much in demand as ornamental trees and shrubs because they develop brilliant autumnal colours. The genus includes some 65 species. Although limited in their native range to the temperate regions of the northern hemisphere, where they are to be found growing wild in wetland, scrub and woodland at up to 2,200 metres (7,218 ft), these days cultivars are familiar in parks and gardens in many parts of the world. *Cornus kousa* originates from eastern parts of Asia, but slightly different varieties are found in Korea, Japan and China so it is also sometimes known as the Chinese, Korean or Japanese dogwood. It differs from the western flowering dogwood, *Cornus florida*, on account of its native range, more upright habit and pointed flower bracts.

The tree is deciduous. Although slow growing at first, it accelerates after several years to reach a maximum of 8–10 metres (26–33 ft) in height with a similar width. Smooth barked, it is strongly branched, often with more than one stem so that it readily presents an open, bushy appearance. Leaves are ovate in shape, thick and papery, initially dark green above and a softer blue-green on the underside, but turning to glorious tints of red and fiery orange in autumn.

The beautiful spectacle of the flowers that unfold in late spring is actually created not from the petals, but with four modified pure white leaves, or bracts, that spread open, pointed and flat, mounted on a slender stalk, collectively creating dense swathes or cymes of between 20 and 40 flowers. The true inner petals are tiny and yellowish-green. In autumn the dark pink-red edible fruits, about 1.5 centimetres (0.6 in) in size, develop as compound globes on long, red stalks and look rather similar to dangling strawberries. In the Far East, they have sometimes been used to make wine.

One of the more bizarre explanations of the name 'dogwood' is that the tree emits a smell attracting dogs to urinate near it, marking their territory. In the 16th century, however, it may have been called a 'dag-wood tree', from an old English word *dag* meaning to pierce, or stab. The species is generally resistant to disease and it produces hard, white wood that was once used in the manufacture of skewers.

KOUSA DOGWOOD

Deciduous

NATIVE TO *Japan, Korea*
HEIGHT *10 m (33 ft)*
TRUNK DIAMETER *0.4 m (1 ft)*
TRUNK GIRTH *1.25 m (4 ft)*
SPREAD *10 m (33 ft)*

ABOVE *The beautiful pure white flowers that unfold in spring consist not of petals, but of modified leaves, or bracts, that surround the minute but true flower parts.*

LEFT *Among the most popular of ornamental trees, this fine specimen of kousa dogwood stands in all its October finery in the gardens of the British Royal Horticultural Society at Wisley.*

HAZEL

Corylus avellana

Hazel is surely one of the more delightful heralds of the European springtime when it shows off its tumbling, delicate cascades of golden catkins. Once the catkins have faded the hazel becomes a rather drab individual, but as the autumn unfolds, it offers up new treasures in its nuts or 'cobs', much favoured by squirrels and other woodland creatures and by the makers of certain chocolate bars.

A small deciduous tree or shrub growing in woodlands throughout temperate Europe and Asia, the hazel can reach a height of 8 metres (26 ft) or more and has for centuries been a familiar component of the lowland hedgerows enclosing the traditional fields of England. The leaves are softly hairy on both sides, rounded, and with a serrated outline.

The hazel relies not on insects but on air currents for its pollination, and so before the leaves unfold in springtime it displays its male catkins, looking like little dangly lambs' tails, which catch the breeze and send their cargoes of pollen to the tiny inconspicuous female flowers that develop on the same tree. Hazel wood is of long-standing economic value, employed for centuries in the manufacture of hurdles and fences. Coppicing, a technique that goes back some 7,000 years, involves the cutting of the tree down to a stump in order that multiple stems will be stimulated to regrow as straight 'poles'. Traditionally, these are harvested every eight years on St John's Day, 23rd June, and are then woven into what is known as wattle. Much of the coppicing of hazel has died out as other materials have overtaken it in popularity, but evidence of this bygone industry is still not difficult to find in woodlands.

Forked hazel twigs or 'wands' have also gained a somewhat esoteric reputation as devices for water divining. In ways that we do not fully understand but that have always possessed magical connotations, the diviner holds the tips of the forks lightly and allegedly they twist as underground water is neared. William Lilly, one of the notable astrologers of 17th-century England, gained a formidable reputation through his use of these divining rods. For many children in the 19th century, hazelnuts became the fore-runners of marbles, and their game was known as 'cobs'.

The Celts revered the magic of the hazel for rather different reasons, because they associated the tree with fertility and wisdom. At midsummer, cattle were once driven through fires and their backs singed by smouldering hazel rods that were then carried by the herdsmen until the following season.

HAZEL

Deciduous

NATIVE TO *Temperate Europe, Asia*
HEIGHT *8 m (26 ft)*
TRUNK DIAMETER *0.4 m (1 ft)*
TRUNK GIRTH *1.25 m (4 ft)*
SPREAD *8 m (26 ft)*

ABOVE *The familiar 'cob' nuts ripen in clusters at the onset of winter to provide vital fare for many small woodland creatures.*

LEFT *Evidence of the bygone industry of coppicing hazel to make poles for hurdles and fences is not hard to find in many old woodlands.*

RED FLOWERING GUM

Corymbia ficifolia

Occasionally, a real gem of a tree emerges from a very small native range and then becomes one of the most popular of ornamentals on account of some special feature – in this case, its brilliantly eye-catching flowers. Red flowering gum is not a true gum and is only found growing in the wild in an area of less than 62 square miles (100 sq km) just inland from the coast of Western Australia, southeast of the city of Perth.

Red flowering gum used to be placed in the true gum or *Eucalyptus* genus but three species, all from Western Australia, including this and one of its closely related cousins, *Corymbia calophylla*, the marri tree, have now been moved to a separate family of 'bloodwoods'. The name refers not to the hue of the timber, which is honey-coloured and often used for furniture making, but to the blood-red colour of the gum or *kino* that readily oozes from wounds in the bark. The two species are difficult to tell apart until they blossom, although the marri generally grows much bigger, sometimes reaching 50 metres (164 ft) in the wild. The red flowering gum is a comparatively small tree, rarely exceeding 10 metres (33 ft) in height, although it can reach 15 metres (49 ft) in cultivation. It is fast growing and has become one of the most widely planted of all the flowering gums in Australia and beyond. It fares well in urban environments and copes with air pollution from vehicle exhausts.

It is found growing naturally in a very small area of open forest just off the coast in the Stirling range of hills near the old colonial port of Albany, Australia, and for this reason it is locally referred to as the Albany red flowering gum. The appearance of the tree is sometimes described as 'straggly', with rough, longitudinally furrowed and fibrous bark clothing the trunk and limbs. The bark, however, is not shed annually in the way that it flakes off in the true gums. The foliage is dark, glossy green and the leaves are ovate or broadly lance shaped with smooth edges and pointed tips.

The flowers are borne outside the leaf canopy in massed bunches at the ends of the branches in what are botanically termed peduncles. They are red or sometimes pinkish-orange, with their most obvious feature being starbursts of long, prominent stamens. These make dazzling displays from January through to early summer. The flowers of the marri are similar but whitish-cream. Pollination is facilitated by birds feeding off the nectar, and the fruits that result from fertilization are woody capsules, shaped like little vases or urns.

RED FLOWERING GUM

Deciduous

NATIVE TO *Coastal southwest Australia*
HEIGHT *10 m (33 ft)*
TRUNK DIAMETER *0.8 m (3 ft)*
TRUNK GIRTH *2.5 m (8 ft)*
SPREAD *10 m (33 ft)*

ABOVE *The flowers erupt during the first part of the year in dazzling starbursts of brilliant red stamens.*

LEFT *A tiny area of Western Australia provides the native home for this beautiful tree. It is now extensively cultivated as an ornamental and this one stands in a field at Marrawah in Tasmania.*

CANNONBALL TREE

Couroupita guianensis

The seemingly implausable name of this tropical evergreen was first earned from a French botanist, J.F. Aublet, who came across the tree in its native South America in 1775 and was struck by the sight of the massive globular fruits that hang in festoons, displaying all the appearance of brown cannonballs. The analogy is heightened by the loud, cracking explosion heard when the fruit drops to the ground and splits open on impact, thus releasing the seeds.

Native to the margins of the Amazonian rainforest, and related to the Brazil nut tree, this is a moderately large species reaching up to 28 metres (92 ft) in height. The tree has a rather untidy appearance, with straggly branches bearing simple, narrowly ovate leaves. Now planted extensively in parks and gardens throughout the warmer regions of the globe, its claim to popularity as an ornamental has come partly from interest in its bizarre fruits but equally from the dazzling, scented flowers that arise in great showy bunches of orange, scarlet and pink blossoms. Its colourful waxy blooms, however, do not arise from new stems as in most plants, but directly from the bark on the trunk and older main branches, in an arrangement botanically known as cauliflory. The flowers may thus cover almost the entire trunk.

Attractive particularly to carpenter bees for their pollen, since they contain no nectar, the flowers are designed to be cross-pollinated by visiting insects and are quite dramatic in appearance. Framed by an arrangement of six deeply pink petals, each flower carries a prominent swathe of false stamens or staminodes. These produce no pollen but arch like a hood over the female ovary and style, surrounded by the small, white and much reduced true stamens. Technically known as zygomorphy, the arrangement of the flower parts is one of bilateral symmetry – in other words, with left and right halves divided vertically and mirroring one another.

In common with a surprising number of other plants and fungi, the cannonball tree relies on animal dispersal. In contrast with the sweet aroma of the flowers, the fruit emits a smell when it bursts open that may be obnoxious to the human nose but is decidedly tempting to other creatures. The seeds are immersed in a gelatinous, fleshy pulp that turns blue-green when exposed to the air. The pulp is eaten by animals, chiefly by herds of wild peccaries and domestic pigs, and thus the seeds are dispersed through their droppings.

THE CANNONBALL TREE

Deciduous (briefly)

NATIVE TO *South America*
HEIGHT *28 m (92 ft)*
TRUNK DIAMETER *0.8 m (3 ft)*
TRUNK GIRTH *2.5 m (8 ft)*
SPREAD *23 m (75 ft)*

ABOVE *The dramatically showy orange-red flowers of the cannonball tree contain no nectar and are pollinated by visiting carpenter bees.*

LEFT *The tree's bizarre appearance is brought about because the large globular fruits are borne in clusters directly on the trunk of the tree.*

COMMON HAWTHORN
Crataegus monogyna

This small tree is a familiar sight in our hedgerows, especially in the latter part of spring when it erupts in a sea of fragrant and delicate pure white flowers that give it the popular name 'mayblossom'. The name 'hawthorn' comes from its spiny armament and the dark red fruits or 'haws' that it bears in autumn. Legend has it that during a pilgrimage to England, Joseph of Arimethea stuck his hawthorn staff into the ground at Glastonbury, where it promptly took root.

Growing rapidly to a maximum height of 15 metres (49 ft), with a dense habit and tolerant of a range of soil conditions and human treatment, hawthorn has been a staple hedgerow plant in England since the first Enclosure Act of the 18th century. Its stout thorns render it especially valuable as a stock-proof barrier, and the trunks are traditonally split and laid to increase its resistance to would-be escapee livestock.

The tree typically develops a dense crown of interlaced branches arising from a short trunk, clothed with smallish, deeply lobed deciduous leaves, arranged in spirals on long stems. Older trees tend to spread more horizontally. The pretty flowers that emerge in profusion in May and June after the leaves are most commonly white, but also come less frequently in a red variety, and they are pollinated mainly by flies said to be attracted to a perfume that bears faint undertones of rotting meat! The fruits or 'haws', in botanical terms single-seeded pomes, make an abundant source of food for birds stocking up before winter, and the birds' subsequent droppings provide the tree with an efficient dispersal mechanism.

When it is not in flower, hawthorn can be a rather inconspicuous small tree or shrub ranging over the length of Europe and into northwest Africa and western Asia. It can also achieve great longevity and there exists a specimen in a churchyard in France that, although there is no scientific proof, allegedly goes back to the 3rd century CE. The original Glastonbury Thorn, which according to legend was 'planted' by Joseph of Arimethea, has long since departed, but cultivars that are supposed to have come from it display the unusual habit of flowering not only in May but again in midwinter. One of the oldest surviving hawthorn trees in Britain, near Brecon Ash in Norfolk, is believed to be about 700 years old. The longevity of the tree can be assisted by its ability to regenerate stems from the base of an old trunk after it is cut down or coppiced.

COMMON HAWTHORN

Deciduous

NATIVE TO *Europe, western Asia, northwest Africa*
HEIGHT *15 m (49 ft)*
TRUNK DIAMETER *1 m (3 ft)*
TRUNK GIRTH *3 m (10 ft)*
SPREAD *14 m (46 ft)*

ABOVE *The glossy red 'haw' fruits hang in clusters, providing much-needed winter sustenance for hungry birds and small mammals.*

LEFT *A hawthorn blasted and disfigured by fierce winter winds stands in solitude amid a winter landscape in the Exmoor National Park, in the southwest of England.*

CHINESE FIR

Cunninghamia lanceolata

A tall and stately evergreen bearing cones and soft needle-like foliage, *Cunninghamia* was once erroneously thought to be related to yew. It is now, however, regarded as the most primitive surviving member of the *Cupressus* family of trees. Although commonly called a 'Chinese fir', it is not a true fir. Its original native range is unknown, because it has been spread extensively throughout much of southeast Asia, where its great height often dominates the forest skylines.

The species was named after an 18th-century English surgeon, James Cunningham, who came across it on a trip to China in 1701. Although Cunningham, who worked for the East India Company, is credited with first describing the tree, specimens did not arrive in the West for more than another hundred years when the botanist William Kerr brought seedlings back to the Royal Botanic Garden at Kew in 1804. It is now to be found growing as an ornamental tree in many European parks. Throughout China, Japan and other countries of the region, the tree is cultivated extensively for economic reasons, much valued for its soft-scented timber. It is logged for building construction and often used in the manufacture of coffins, since the wood is resistant to both fungal and insect attack. Grown on mountain slopes, it can cope with altitudes up to 2,500 metres (8,202 ft).

When fully matured in the wild, an individual specimen can soar to 50 metres (164 ft), dominating all other trees. Carried up on a single, straight, massive trunk, the limbs are clothed in reddish bark fissured lengthwise, which tends to peel away in flakes. Narrow and fairly open at the crown, the spreading lower branches can extend to 9 metres (30 ft), drooping elegantly at their extremities, and bearing long, shiny, soft but sharp-pointed needles, arranged in flat spirals around the stems. The needles are green in spring and summer but turn a pretty shade of bronze through the autumn and winter months, reminiscent of a *Cryptomeria*. Each needle is decorated with two distinctive white bands of breathing stomata on the underside, and unless damaged by frost can live on the tree for as long as five years before it falls. The inner boughs can carry quite a volume of dead needles that may make the foliage look somewhat untidy on close inspection.

The inflorescence of each sex is borne on the same tree. The tiny male flowers erupt in clusters in May at the tips of the stems, while the females are borne singly and develop into rounded or rosette shapes quite unlike the more familiar barrel-shaped cones of true firs.

CHINESE FIR

Evergreen

NATIVE TO *China, Taiwan, Vietnam*
HEIGHT *50 m (164 ft)*
TRUNK DIAMETER *3 m (10 ft)*
TRUNK GIRTH *9.5 m (31 ft)*
SPREAD *12 m (39 ft)*

ABOVE *A cluster of Chinese firs stands tall and stately in a forested valley near Hong Kong.*

LEFT *The fruits of the Chinese fir develop with the appearance of little green rosebuds, very different to the familiar cones of many other conifers.*

CHINESE WEEPING CYPRESS

Cupressus funebris

It is not too difficult to see why this tree is so named. Its branches curve down in dense, pendulous swathes and instantly conjure up a tranquil air of sadness and solitude. The gracious, weeping appearance of this evergreen has made it a firm favourite in parks and ornamental gardens throughout the warmer temperate regions of the world, and in bygone days in China it was regularly planted in the vicinity of temples and shrines.

Not least because the Chinese weeping cypress has been in cultivation for virtually as long as recorded history, it now difficult to establish exactly where its original native range lay. It prefers life in limestone areas on mountain slopes up to altitudes of 1,100 metres (3,609 ft) and today it has been recorded growing in the wild in a wide spectrum of forests through central and southwest China. It is tolerant of some degree of frost and can also cope with heat and drought. Some of the trees achieve great longevity: a specimen standing beside the Black Dragon Pool Mountain Temple near Kunming in Yunnan province is reportedly at least 800 years of age.

So long as the tree has reasonable living space and is not crowded by others, it runs to a medium size, at most reaching a height of 30 metres (98 ft) and generally less, but with a stout trunk of up to 2 metres (7 ft) across. In a mature tree the branches sweep outwards, arising more or less from the base of the trunk, the lowest limbs tending to brush the ground in an arrangement botanically known as decumbent, before ascending slightly. The little branchlets borne at their tips are densely clothed and pendulous, falling like tears. It is cultivated extensively as an ornamental both in southern China and beyond.

A young, immature tree bears needles arranged in small whorls along the stems. As the tree matures, the form of the foliage changes and becomes scale like with little flat, greyish-green leaves closely pressed to the stems. The leaves contain pairs of glands that, when crushed or rubbed, release an aroma of freshly mown grass.

The male cones are very small and inconspicuous, shedding their pollen into the breeze in the early spring to fertilize the female cones; the female cones are rounded in shape, green at first and becoming dark brown when ripe, in the late summer two years after pollination. The scales open to release their tiny, flattened, shiny brown seeds.

CHINESE WEEPING CYPRESS

Evergreen

NATIVE TO *Southwest and central China*
HEIGHT *30 m (98 ft)*
TRUNK DIAMETER *2 m (7 ft)*
TRUNK GIRTH *6.25 m (21 ft)*
SPREAD *28 m (92 ft)*

ABOVE *The small female cones, at first green before they ripen, hang in pom-pom clusters from the ends of the branches.*

LEFT *With sweeping, pendulous branches giving this tree a sorrowful yet tranquil air, the Chinese weeping cypress is often planted near temples.*

RIMU

Dacrydium cupressinum

The rimu is a veritable giant of a southern hemisphere conifer, native to the forests of New Zealand. When full grown, it can tower into the sky far above other trees that make up the forest canopy. Regularly reaching 50 metres (164 ft) into the sky, there are reports of some specimen trees, whch have since been felled, even reaching in excess of 60 metres (197 ft), having survived for more than 900 years.

A true giant of the rainforests, the rimu grows very slowly and its outline changes as it matures. As a young tree, it adopts a conical profile with its branches bowing down in a weeping habit. When fully grown, however, the trunk becomes virtually bare of branches for three-quarters of its length and those left at the crown spread out more horizontally so that it appears round topped, with little terminal branchlets that hang down somewhat at their tips. The arrangement of the needle-like leaves also changes from youth to old age. For many years on younger trees, the needles overlap spirally around the stems, but stand out with sharp tips. As the tree ages, the needles get smaller, more bluntly tipped, and become closely pressed against the branches. The bark of the straight main trunk is brownish-grey and tends to peel off in long flakes.

Remains of the ancestors of rimu can be found in fossil beds dating back 70 million years, and at one time it was probably the most dominant species in those prehistoric landscapes. Today when growing in the wild, it is still very widespread throughout New Zealand, both in farmland and ascending forested lower mountain slopes to about 600 metres (1,969 ft). Some of the tallest surviving specimens are to be found in the Pureora Forest Park, a vast conservation area in the centre of the North Island where their felling is prohibited. Seeds of the rimu were first collected by the botanist Joseph Banks, who accompanied Captain Cook on his initial voyage to the antipodes in 1770, and today the tree is grown as an ornamental not only in New Zealand but also in many other parts of the world.

A member of the Podocarp family, the rimu has separate male and female trees. In the female the cones, produced only once in every five or six years, become reduced to a few fleshy scales that, in botanical terms, are highly modified terminal leaves. These form a swollen receptacle surrounding the seed. Birds feast on the attractive fleshy parts and hence pass the seeds out in their droppings.

RIMU

Evergreen

NATIVE TO *New Zealand*
HEIGHT *50 m (164 ft)*
TRUNK DIAMETER *1.8 m (6 ft)*
TRUNK GIRTH *5.6 m (18 ft)*
SPREAD *28 m (92 ft)*

ABOVE *The young, spiky leaves of the rimu stand out, sharp-tipped, from the stems.*

LEFT *The ancestry of these colossal trees extends back 70 million years in their native New Zealand home, but today they are planted in many parts of the world as ornamentals.*

HANDKERCHIEF TREE

Davidia involucrata

This delightful tree is best known for its large, papery flowers, which resemble fluttering handkerchiefs – or, if one uses one's imagination, white doves, for which reason it is also popularly called the 'dove tree'. Its discovery in China at the turn of the last century was marked by a bizarre series of mishaps, but specimen plants eventually reached Europe and North America in 1904 and it has since become hugely popular as an ornamental.

A deciduous tree that grows to a middling height of not more than 25 metres (82 ft), generally less, with a broadly triangular outline, its branches are clothed with heart-shaped ovate leaves on red stalks that look not dissimilar to the foliage of a lime or basswood tree. Two very similar subspecies are cultivated, one of which has fine hairs on the undersides of the leaves and is the hardier of the two, while the other is hairless.

The most striking features of *Davidia* are undoubtedly the flowers. These do not appear until the tree is at least ten years old and sometimes older, but then create a truly dazzling display during the month of May. The actual infloresence is quite small and built like a tightly clustered pom-pom, yellowish-green and equipped with purple anthers. The flower heads that erupt in great masses along the branches each then become framed by two large leafy bracts that are pure white and of unequal proportions, one roughly twice the size of the other, and as much as 25 centimetres (10 in) long. The bracts hang down, butterfly-like, in long rows fluttering ceaselessly in the breeze. The fruit is a comparatively unremarkable dark green ridged nut that turns purple when ripe. About 3 centimetres (1 in) across, each fruit dangles from a long, 10-centimetre (4-in) stalk.

Davidia is named after the French naturalist and Vincentian missionary Père Armand David, who spent most of his working life in China from 1862 onwards and died in 1900. David first described the tree and collected seeds in 1868. These, however, were lost when the boat carrying them down the Han river capsized in rapids. Another plant hunter, Augustine Henry, later came across a *Davidia* growing in one of the gorges of the Yangtse river but only noted its presence. Then in 1899 a third entrepreneur, the 22-year-old Ernest Wilson, set out to find the tree, equipped with Henry's hand-drawn sketch map and knowing none of the language, only to discover that it had been felled. He managed to collect seeds but these, too, were lost when his own boat capsized in treacherous rapids. However, he retraced his steps to pick up replacements and sent the seeds safely to England in 1901. The first tree grown in an English garden flowered in 1911.

HANDKERCHIEF TREE

Deciduous

NATIVE TO *Central and southwest China*
HEIGHT *25 m (82 ft)*
TRUNK DIAMETER *0.6 m (2 ft)*
TRUNK GIRTH *1.8 m (6 ft)*
SPREAD *23 m (75 ft)*

ABOVE *The bracts form a backdrop to the spherical fruits, which mature from minute, inconspicuous flowers.*

LEFT *One of the prettiest of deciduous trees, the species came originally from China but is now grown extensively as an ornamental or for its large, creamy, handkerchief-like bracts.*

ROYAL POINCIANA

Delonix regia

If any single member of the world's families of trees deserves the ultimate accolade for its sheer, vibrant beauty or 'wow factor', the 'flame tree' or royal poinciana must surely be a serious contender. Native to the dry, deciduous forests of the island of Madagascar in the Indian Ocean, it is now cultivated throughout the tropical regions of the world and is regularly voted to be in the top five most stunning floral trees.

Curiously, although *Delonix regia* has been in extensive cultivation since the 19th century, any knowledge of where it originated was lost to science until it was rediscovered growing in the wilds of northern and western Madagascar in the 1930s. Sadly it is now on the verge of extinction in its native range, where it has fallen victim to decades of felling in order to make charcoal, but it thrives in cultivation from India to Hawaii and Australia, and is commonly planted along urban streets and in parks and gardens.

A comparatively small deciduous tree preferring to be sited in full sun, it grows to little more than 15 metres (49 ft) with a thick, buttressed trunk and smooth, greyish-brown bark. The horizontally spreading branches give the tree an umbrella shape, making it appear wider than it is tall, and the branches are clothed with feathery, fern or mimosa-like leaves. These are light green, and have up to 25 pairs of oppositely arranged pinnate leaflets. They fall in the dry season to be replaced more or less immediately by new foliage. As a member of the legume family, the flame tree is related to mimosas and tamarinds and, like mimosa, its leaves close up and go to sleep when darkness falls.

As the new leaves appear, the tree erupts in great masses of exotic, flaming-red blossoms in such profusion that they virtually obscure the green foliage and the tree appears from a distance to be one single, scarlet fire. Each flower is 12 centimetres (5 in) or more across, and opens to reveal a tuft of stamens and five broad, spoon-shaped petals, one 'banner petal' being larger than the rest. Each petal turns in on itself at the tip like a claw and the petals are attended by five smaller yellow and red sepals. When the fertilized flowers shrivel away, the fruit takes the form of a greenish, flat bean pod up to 70 centimetres (28 in) long containing the seeds, which turns brown and woody as it ripens.

ROYAL POINCIANA

Deciduous

NATIVE TO *Madagascar*
HEIGHT *15 m (49 ft)*
TRUNK DIAMETER *0.65 m (2 ft)*
TRUNK GIRTH *2 m (7 ft)*
SPREAD *17 m (56 ft)*

ABOVE *Standing here on a skyline near Oaxaca in Mexico, the royal poinciana has become a firm ornamental favourite far from its native home in Madagascar.*

LEFT *Also known for obvious reasons as the flame tree, the species bears mimosa-like leaves, gorgeous red blossoms, and large, distinctive fruit pods.*

SOUTH AFRICAN WILD PEAR

Dombeya rotundifolia

Some trees have collected inappropriate common names. *Dombeya rotundifolia* bears no relation to the tree that yields edible pears, *Pyrus communis,* and which is a member of the Rosaceae family. The *Dombeya* species, of which there are over 250, belong to the Malvaceae and, in common with other members of the mallow family, many bear exquisitely beautiful displays of scented blossoms in springtime. The South African wild pear is so called only because the flowers are said to resemble those of the common pear.

A small, fast-growing deciduous tree, *Dombeya rotundifolia* rarely achieves a height of more than 10 metres (33 ft) and generally much less, so in some respects may be thought of as a large flowering shrub. The genus earned the name *Dombeya* in honour of an 18th-century French botanist, Joseph Dombey, who spent much of his working life in South America and whose botanical collection in London still stands as one of the most valuable herbarium records of Chilean and Peruvian plants outside South America.

The native range of the South African wild pear is chiefly in the southern half of the continent, from South Africa extending up the central and eastern regions towards Ethiopia. It prefers to make its home on deep alluvial soils along river banks, although it will also thrive on rocky hillsides up to altitudes of 1,200 metres (3,937 ft) and has been known to select vantage points atop termite mounds. The tree rises on a fairly slender dark greyish-brown trunk that sometimes branches from the base and spreads into a rounded, fairly open crown. The bark can become quite deeply fissured lengthwise and corky with age, when the blackish cork layer acts as a natural protective sheath against fire damage. Leaves are leathery in texture; their rounded shape lends to the epithet *rotundifolia*. They unfold covered densely in tiny star-shaped or stellate hairs that are a characteristic feature of the *Dombeya* genus, most of whose members are confined in their native range to the island of Madagascar in the Indian Ocean.

The crowning glory of the tree is unquestionably its mass of star-shaped blossoms, which emerge before the leaves in springtime in a blaze of white and occasionally pastel pink clusters, properly termed panicles, and are then pollinated by insects attracted by the abundant nectar. Unusually, the remnants of the flowers remain on the tree for some time, and when the fruit has developed in the form of little capsules, the dead petals detach and act as wings to carry the fruits away from the tree before the seeds are liberated.

SOUTH AFRICAN WILD PEAR

Deciduous

NATIVE TO *South and east Africa*
HEIGHT *10 m (33 ft)*
TRUNK DIAMETER *0.4 m (1 ft)*
TRUNK GIRTH *1.25 m (4 ft)*
SPREAD *8 m (26 ft)*

ABOVE *The flowers are packed in dense clusters of white and pink star-shaped blooms.*

LEFT *A member of the mallow family, this pretty tree in the Matobo Hills of South Africa erupts in creamy, scented blossoms before its leaves unfold.*

COAST CORAL TREE

Erythrina caffra

No book with a title such as *The Beauty of Trees* would be complete without proper mention of coral trees and the sheer exotic magnificence of their blooms. The coast coral tree is one of five South African species in a genus that also includes the common coral tree and the cockspur coral tree, each of which bears large, bright red and exceptionally showy flowers.

The native range of the coast coral tree, so called because of its coral-red flowers, lies in southeast Africa, in which another of its common names is the 'kafferboom'. It tends to favour positions on the edges of forests near the coast and along inland river valleys. However, it is now so widely cultivated for its ornamental value that it has become the official tree of the city of Los Angeles in California. Worldwide there are more than 110 different species of coral trees, distributed across both Old and New World regions, with about half of them found in Mexico and Central America.

Coast coral is a deciduous tree that grows to a medium height of 20 metres (66 ft) or less with a straight, grey trunk and a spreading, open canopy. The trees tend, however, not to be particularly long lived. They are fast growing with substantial rooting systems, but the wood of the trunk and limbs is weak and prone to collapse. Among the biggest specimens are those standing in South Africa's vast Addo Elephant National Park in the Eastern Cape.

The young branches of all the *Erythrina* species are armed with small thorns not unlike those on a rosebush, but as the limb matures these are sloughed off. The tree bears light green trifoliate leaves, meaning that they unfold on a long stalk with three broadly ovate leaflets. The central leaflet is larger than the other two and each has a pointed tip and narrow base.

The main flowering of the coast coral tree takes place in early spring, but it will then continue to produce blossoms sporadically for much of the rest of the year. The blooms are truly exotic in appearance, arising in dense clusters at the tips of branches. The individual corolla or flower tube is made up of five petals – one large standard that becomes separated from the others when the flower is mature, two elongated keel petals that are fused together, and two small lateral or wing petals. The male stamens form a sheath of ten that surround the female parts and pollination is mainly carried out by hummingbirds feeding off the copious nectar. The seeds are bright red with thick, impervious coats and can thus be carried for long distances on ocean currents that aid dispersal.

COAST CORAL TREE

Deciduous

NATIVE TO *Southeast Africa*
HEIGHT *20 m (66 ft)*
TRUNK DIAMETER *0.5 m (2 ft)*
TRUNK GIRTH *1.6 m (5 ft)*
SPREAD *18 m (59 ft)*

ABOVE *Commencing its flowering season in early spring and continuing for many months, the most eye-catching feature of the blooms is their large, elongated keel petals.*

LEFT *The exotic magnificence of the red blossoms decorating this tree growing on the lower slopes of Mount Kilimanjaro in Tanzania would be hard to miss.*

RED RIVER GUM

Eucalyptus camaldulensis

This majestic tree is so called, not after a river of that name, but because of the colour of its wood, which can range from palest pink through brilliant reds to almost black depending on the age of the timber and the amount of weathering. Red river gum is probably the most widely encountered of all the 800 or so species of gum trees. It is found mainly in Australia and Africa, although it has been planted in many other parts of the world.

Red river gum is a substantial evergreen tree that can grow to 45 metres (148 ft) in height on a trunk that is often misshapen and spreads into a broad, open and rather ragged canopy of irregular and twisted branches, bearing dense foliage. The bark possesses a fairly characteristic white-grey appearance, sometimes with pink- or buff-tinged patches, and it can peel away in sheets near the trunk base. The base may also develop adventitious prop roots angling down into the soil from above ground level to assist with support on flood plains. Foliage is carried on long, slender, drooping twigs that are reddish in colour, and the leaves are narrow, glossy and grey-green. Sometimes more than 25 centimetres (10 in) long, each tapers to an elongated point and may have a curved profile.

One of the more sinister local names of the species is the 'widow maker', on account of its habit, possibly as a means of conserving water during periods of drought, of pruning itself at intervals when massive limbs can break away without warning. The wood, however, is notably brittle. Red river gum can cope with wide-ranging conditions within tropical, subtropical and milder temperate regions, although it tends to favour life near water. It can tolerate regular flooding and it is thus found along the margins of many Australian rivers. One of its major remaining natural refuges is a sizeable 65,000-hectare (160,618-acre) forest bordering the states of Victoria and New South Wales, the Barmah-Millewa Forest, in which it remains the dominant tree species. Elsewhere, its native range has been drastically reduced by unregulated logging.

The flowers are borne on slender stalks arising from the axils of the leaves and form white clusters, or umbels, each with tufts of multiple stamens surrounding the female parts, but with an absence of petals. In bud, the flowers are protected by a curious arrangement in which the top of the pedicel or flower stalk is invaginated to surround the developing flower parts. Pollination is then by wind. Red river gum can be distinguished from related species by the shape of its yellowish-brown seed capsules, which are hemispherical with a prominent beak that opens in a criss-cross pattern when ripe to release the seeds.

RED RIVER GUM

Evergreen

NATIVE TO *Australia*
HEIGHT *45 m (148 ft)*
TRUNK DIAMETER *2 m (7 ft)*
TRUNK GIRTH *6.25 m (21 ft)*
SPREAD *40 m (131 ft)*

ABOVE *The white clusters of flowers are oddly constructed so that the top of each flower stalk grows around to encase the developing flower.*

LEFT *A true gum tree, the red river gum, seen here growing on the banks of the Murray river in Australia, is so called because of the often brilliant red colour of its timber.*

Red river gums glow red against the evening sky in the Flinders Range in Southern Australia.

CIDER GUM
Eucalyptus gunnii

All eucalyptus trees 'breathe' the spirit of Crocodile Dundee, aboriginal walkabouts and the hot, dusty Australian bush, but cider gum has also become very popular as an ornamental tree in places far beyond its local ranges in Australia and Tasmania. This is because it is fairly tolerant of colder conditions, thrives in most soils, and grows quickly to show off its pretty, waxy, bluish-green evergreen foliage.

The biggest eucalyptus species can grow to more than 90 metres (295 ft) tall and thus rival the other forest giants like the Douglas fir and coast redwood. Cider gum, however, is a comparative minnow, rarely reaching skywards much beyond 35 metres (115 ft) in the wild. For a long time the tree was strictly native to Tasmania, growing on the island's central plateau up to around 1,100-metre (3,609-ft) altitudes, but in the distant past it became well established in many parts of the Australian highlands and there are now thought to be more of these trees planted outside Tasmania than surviving on the island istelf. One of the oldest introduced specimen trees now stands on the South Island of New Zealand and is thought to be about 100 years old. Cider gum was first introduced to Europe in the mid-1850s and is considered to be tolerant of most cold winters in lowland regions, and when planted against southwest-facing slopes.

Growing in the wild with a fairly narrowly cone-shaped outline at rates of up to 1.5 metres (5 ft) a year, the straight trunk shows off pretty cream and greyish-pink bark that, in common with that of most eucalypts, readily peels away each year in big flakes. Older trees become broader, with heavy, spreading branches.

Aside from its decorative bark, the evergreen leaves are the tree's most attractive feature. With a glaucous or waxy surface, designed to minimize water loss in arid environments, they vary in shape according to the tree's age. In young plants each leaf is somewhat rounded in shape and blue-green, but as the tree matures, the shape and colour of the leaves changes so that they become greener and more elongated. The foliage also gives off a distinctive aromatic perfume, especially in hot sun. The white flowers, delicate though not particularly eye catching, bloom in midsummer.

The curious name 'cider gum' has been earned from the past use of the sap among Tasmanian aboriginals to make a traditional alcoholic beverage. If the sap, which has high sugar content, is collected in spring and then kept in a closed container, it ferments to a brew that tastes not unlike apple cider.

CIDER GUM

Evergreen

NATIVE TO *Australia*
HEIGHT *35 m (115 ft)*
TRUNK DIAMETER *1.5 m (5 ft)*
TRUNK GIRTH *4.7 m (15 ft)*
SPREAD *32 m (105 ft)*

ABOVE *The tiny flowers, small but perfectly formed, are made up of masses of delicate stamens concealing almost non-existent petals.*

LEFT *The unusual angle of this photograph shows off the pretty cream bark that peels away annually in great, flaky strips.*

COMMON BEECH

Fagus sylvatica

Familiar surely to almost everyone living in the temperate regions of Europe, from Scandinavia to the Mediterranean as far east as Turkey, the beech has to be one of our favourite deciduous trees. It bears unprepossessing flowers and fruits, but the absence of gaudiness is more than compensated for in its fine, broadly spreading shape and soft green foliage. The tree creates an indelible impression across so many of our lowland landscapes.

The species is comparatively slow growing and, when allowed to mature unrestricted by other competitors in open areas, the common beech can achieve considerable size, ascending to more than 45 metres (148 ft) in height. It possesses a straight and sturdy trunk clothed with generally smooth, light grey bark. Although when sharing space in dense woodland individual trees can be squeezed into a quite narrow profile, with most of the branches at the top, in more open areas or in isolation they will keep more of the lower branches and spread out to make broad and elegant crowns.

The trees develop only shallow root systems that do not anchor them particularly well, and for this reason the bigger specimens are prone to toppling in strong winds. Nonetheless, the average lifespan of a beech is up to 200 years and veteran trees are known to have survived for 300 years before succumbing to the ravages of old age. Historically, many of the trees have tended to be pollarded for their timber.

A beech tree bears a dense canopy of leaves, delicately pale green and pubescent at first, later smooth and of darker hue. This mass of foliage excludes much of the sunlight from the forest floor throughout the summer, and so while the surface of a beech wood is generally thickly carpeted with deep layers of litter, it may be devoid of much other vegetation. When the last of the gold-tinted autumn colour has abandoned the tree, exposing the wispy tips of the horizontal branches, they are seen to curve upwards like so many graceful fingers carrying long, slender, overwintering buds covered in brown scales.

In Europe the beech does not bear flowers until it is at least 30 years of age, often much older, and these take the form of tiny male and female catkins that appear after the leaves in late spring. Pollination takes place through the action of the wind. The seeds or 'beechmast' are triangular nuts protected by bristly husks that split open to release the seeds when they fall to the ground in autumn, and these provide abundant late-season fare for birds, squirrels and other woodland mammals.

COMMON BEECH

Deciduous

NATIVE TO *Europe*
HEIGHT *45 m (148 ft)*
TRUNK DIAMETER *3 m (10 ft)*
TRUNK GIRTH *9.5 m (31 ft)*
SPREAD *45 m (148 ft)*

ABOVE *The young leaves of beech are not dissimilar to those of hornbeam, but are uniquely soft and covered in downy hairs.*

LEFT *The spreading beech graces woodlands throughout Europe, where it provides both food and refuge for a host of small creatures as the summer departs and green turns to gold.*

WEEPING BEECH

Fagus sylvatica var. *pendula*

If graceful style and evocative shape are to be any measure of beauty in a tree, then this cultivated variety of the standard native European beech must be a strong contender for the highest accolade, alongside the weeping willow. Its sweeping, pendulous limbs and rich foliage always offer the eye a bittersweet mix of sorrow and joy. In common with the standard tree, it also has a glorious copper-red leaved variety.

The weeping variety of the beech was introduced to European parks and gardens at some time during the 1830s and has since been exported to North America. The edges of ornamental lakes have become some of the favourite spots for planting these trees, where their reflection in still water can create such a magical effect. Because of their cascading habit the trees do not grow to the same height as the standard European beech, reaching at most 25 metres (82 ft) tall, but they can spread majestically. Where the branches touch the ground they are able to put out roots, and thus a specimen tree can sometimes finish up with a width that exceeds its height. The tree reaches maturity after about 100 years and requires a goodly amount of living space in order to achieve its full potential. Not excessively long lived, however, the oldest specimens rarely survive much beyond 150 years of age.

Weeping beech grows well in most locations, although it does not enjoy exposed positions or salt spray in maritime locations. The trunk and branches of weeping beech are much the same as those of the standard species, aside from the obvious horizontal spreading and cascading of the limbs, though they tend to be more contorted. The colour of the bark tends towards a silvery grey and is generally smooth, but develops fine vertical furrows with age. The leaves also mirror those of the green native tree, aside from their striking colour, which is present from the moment that they first unfold in springtime.

The splendid colour of the copper beech's leaves is worth a brief explanation. It is actually a form of optical illusion. The leaves of all plants contain a range of different pigments, chlorophyll, carotenoids and anthocyanin, which absorb separate wavelengths of the light spectrum. Chlorophyll absorbs red and blue so the leaf appears green to our eyes, but anthocyanins absorb the blue and green parts of the spectrum, giving us a leaf that looks red or purple. Copper beech produces high quantities of anthocyanin in its foliage tissues and thus we perceive the unusual colouration of the leaves.

WEEPING BEECH

Deciduous

NATIVE TO *Europe*
HEIGHT *25 m (82 ft)*
TRUNK DIAMETER *1.5 m (5 ft)*
TRUNK GIRTH *4.7 m (15 ft)*
SPREAD *28 m (92 ft)*

ABOVE *A defining feature of beech leaves lies in the prominent veins that stand out especially as the foliage starts to fade at the end of the summer.*

LEFT *The native beech tree has been hybridized to create beautiful weeping canopies whose cascading branches reach down and brush the ground.*

BANYAN

Ficus benghalensis

At Ramohalli, near the city of Bangalore, stands a venerable banyan specimen that is reputed to be around 400 years old, but its age is unsubstantiated and perhaps the stuff of legend. A mere stripling in comparison, much damaged by disease but spreading over a wider surface area of about 14,500 square metres (47,572 sq ft), the so-called Great Banyan Tree of Kolkata (Calcutta) is more authentically placed at about 250 years of age, thus having put out its first shoots at the time of the coronation of George III in England.

The banyan can grow to a maximum of about 30 metres (98 ft) in height, but technically it can spread *ad infinitum* over a very wide area because of its curious rooting arrangements. In appearance, a banyan of any age is an extraordinary sight because the arrangement of its roots and branches appears topsy-turvy. The trunk puts out adventitious or propagating roots from high up, which then angle downwards and, where they reach the ground, promote the growth of new trunks that then form a circle around the original, spreading further and further as seasons go by. The branches are clothed with glossy ovate leaves that are big and leathery, thus resisting dessication in the intense daytime heat.

If the rooting system is remarkable, so too are the fig's flowering arrangements, because the inflorescence takes the unique form of an enclosed vase-like structure, the cavity of which is lined with tiny flowers. These have to be pollinated by a no-less diminutive and highly specialized insect, the fig wasp, which has the ability to penetrate the vase. The resultant sweet-tasting fruit attracts birds and other animals, and the seeds are dispersed through their droppings. The tree actually germinates from seed as an epiphyte in cracks and crevices of other host trees and even the old mortar of buildings, but the banyan's aerial roots can then effectively smother the host, giving it another popular name of 'strangler fig'.

Sacred to Hindus, the banyan is the national tree of India, and its native range extends throughout much of the subcontinent. The word *banias* means 'salesmen'. This improbable title was earned because the spreading shade of the tree along roadsides has long been a favourite place for hot and dusty merchant travellers to cool off and conduct their business. However, banyans have been cultivated in many other parts of the tropics, and the tree earned literary prestige after Daniel Defoe's fictional hero Robinson Crusoe chose to make his home in a banyan.

BANYAN

Deciduous (briefly)

NATIVE TO *India*
HEIGHT *30 m (98 ft)*
TRUNK DIAMETER *Variable*
TRUNK GIRTH *Variable*
SPREAD *Variable, can be over 100 m (328 ft)*

ABOVE *Banyan fruits, clustered fig-like at the tip of a young branch.*

LEFT *The prop roots of a massive and aged banyan provide their own own dramatic and unique imagery beside a forest track in the Ranthambore National Park in northern India.*

PATAGONIAN CYPRESS

Fitzroya cupressoides

This veritable colossus of a tree stands alone as the only member of its genus, and was first named by Charles Darwin in honour of Robert Fitzroy, the captain of HMS *Beagle*. A plant of tremendous longevity and size, native to the Andes mountains of Chile and Argentina, some specimens in Argentina's Los Alerces National Park around the southern shores of Lake Menendes are reported to be more than 70 metres (230 ft) in height and a massive 16 metres (52 ft) in girth around the base of the trunk.

Known in South America as the alerce, in terms of longevity the Patagonian cypress ranks a close second to the bristlecone pine. In 1993, a count of the growth rings on one massive specimen felled in Chile showed it to be 3,622 years old. It is also one of the world's most ancient arboreal species. Thirty-five-million-year-old fossils have been discovered in Tasmania, indicating that this tree played a major role in the prehistoric Antarctic flora at a time when a land bridge existed between the continents of Australasia and South America.

An evergreen that matures into an untidy conical shape, the trunk and main branches are clothed in reddish bark that flakes off in strips, with smaller terminal branchlets that tend to hang downwards. Stems are clothed with needles in whorls of three, each flattened and lance shaped with a pointed tip, and with the underside marked by two white stomatal strips.

Male and female cones are generally, though not always, borne on separate trees. The male inflorescence is small and nestles in the axils of the needles; the female cone, at first green then brown and woody, is made up of nine scales in three whorls, the lowermost and frequently middle whorl being sterile. Pollination is by wind, and the tiny winged seeds that develop on the scales are also carried on the wind.

The Patagonian cypress is now classed as an endangered species, and its decline in the Patagonian rainforests has come about due to at least one less than obvious factor. Logging has undoubtedly played a detrimental role because the reddish-brown, straight-grained timber has been exploited for its considerable economic value, especially during the 19th and 20th centuries. Even now, although the tree is protected in law, the Chilean authorities find it near-impossible to eradicate illegal logging. However, the tree is also unusually dependent on forest fires that allow for the periodic burning down of old timber and the regeneration of new stands. Modern fire-prevention measures have thus perversely added to its woes.

PATAGONIAN CYPRESS

Evergreen

NATIVE TO *Andes Mountains, South America*
HEIGHT *70 m (230 ft)*
TRUNK DIAMETER *5 m (16 ft)*
TRUNK GIRTH *16 m (52 ft)*
SPREAD *15 m (49 ft)*

ABOVE *The small, dry cones of the Patagonian cypress contain only two or three viable seeds each.*

LEFT *Colossal 70-metre (230-ft) veterans touch the sky in the Alerce Andino National Park, Chile.*

EUROPEAN ASH

Fraxinus excelsior

If a single species of European native tree can claim to embody the character and gnarled wisdom of the ages, it is probably the ash that takes the prize. Unsurprisingly, this imposing tree was chosen in Norse mythology as the Tree of the World, Yggdrasil, whose roots reach deep down to the underworld, drawing on its well of eternal knowledge, and whose grey, massively distorted branches touch the world of the gods. The ash was thus for people in bygone times the stairway between heaven and hell.

Although commonly known as the European ash, the natural range of the species extends into Asia Minor and parts of north Africa. Growing to a maximum of 45 metres (148 ft), though generally nearer 35 metres (115 ft), the tree falls well short of the dimensions of some, although still a large structure. But if it lacks stature in comparative size, it more than makes up for this in character. The tree can live for 150 years, by which time it is a tall, though hardly graceful, tree with a long, deeply fissured trunk and an open canopy. What gives it much of its appeal and sense of mysticism in maturity is the gnarling and crooked disfigurement that so often affects the limbs. An aged ash breathes rugged antiquity.

A young tree, less than 50 years of age, bears few of these gnarled attributes. It possesses a clean, grey bark, devoid of fissures, and its branches, still fairly straight, reach upwards to create a narrowish, forking outline. Only with age and as limbs are progressively ripped off in storms does the extraordinary disfigurement and twisting start to take over.

Ash leaves are compound, made up of opposite pairs of narrow, lance-shaped leaflets, and it is their loosely spaced arrangement that gives the tree its open, airy appearance, even in midsummer. The ash is one of the latest species to come into leaf in springtime and among the earliest to shed its greenery in autumn, virtually unchanged with any autumn tints. So for much of the year the boughs are clearly visible, and the ends of the twigs are characterized in the European ash by dense black buds, which in other *Fraxinus* species are brown or grey.

The trees can be separately male and female or with both sexes on the same plant, the catkins emerging before the leaves. These are small and purplish in colour, and pollination is achieved by wind action. The developing fruits hang in dense bunches in the form of winged seeds or samaras, generally referred to as 'ash keys', that spin to the ground when they are released.

EUROPEAN ASH

Deciduous

NATIVE TO *Europe*
HEIGHT *45 m (148 ft)*
TRUNK DIAMETER *3 m (10 ft)*
TRUNK GIRTH *9.5 m (31 ft)*
SPREAD *35 m (115 ft)*

ABOVE *Winged samaras hang in dense, late-summer bunches ready for release.*

LEFT *The limbs of a mature ash tree become deeply twisted, fractured and distorted, contrasting with the delicate pinnate foliage.*

MAIDENHAIR TREE
Ginkgo biloba

Ginkgo is the nearest tree species to a living fossil, probably tracing back to the early Jurassic era between 200 and 180 million years ago, when its forebears shared living space with dinosaurs. Fossils that appear closely related to the modern ginkgo reach back even further to the Permian period, 270 million years ago. Ginkgos seem to have been reasonably plentiful throughout the Cretaceous period, but they became restricted in their range; by the end of the Pliocene epoch the fossil record dies out, other than within a small area of central China where the modern tree is still to be found.

Discovered in China in 1690 by a German botanist, Engelbert Kaempfer, the ginkgo is our oldest tree species, and it would have commonly been growing in antiquity alongside other early plants including cycads and ferns. It evolved long before any flowering species clothed the Earth, and although its fan-shaped foliage may look similar to that of a broad-leaved deciduous tree, it bears no relationship, and it may indeed provide an evolutionary link between ferns and flowering plants. A living ginkgo may also possess considerable longevity, and in this respect one of the oldest trees standing in Kew Gardens, London, is a male ginkgo that was planted in 1762 under the patronage of George III's mother, Princess Augusta. Alas, it has no mate! The ginkgo is popularly known as a maidenhair tree because the leaves bear a passing resemblance to those on a maidenhair fern.

Gardeners may perceive ginkgos as fairly small trees, but in the wild in China some monster specimens are known to have achieved heights in excess of 50 metres (164 ft). Best suited to life in soil that is both well drained and regularly watered, a young ginkgo grows tall and slim, but as it ages it can develop a broad canopy resting on a massive trunk. Today, it is the national tree of China.

The leaf of the tree is fan shaped, marked with veins that radiate out and branch, and is divided into two lobes, hence the name *biloba*. Ginkgo possesses a very unusual mode of reproduction not seen in any other modern living tree. The primitive male 'pollen', properly known as a gamete, is produced on a separate plant to the female organ and is initially borne on the wind – but when it settles on a female plant, it develops a motile sperm-like ability and literally drags itself to what is properly called a female archegonium in order to complete fertilization.

MAIDENHAIR TREE

Deciduous

NATIVE TO *China*
HEIGHT *35 m (115 ft)*
TRUNK DIAMETER *0.5 m (2 ft)*
TRUNK GIRTH *1.6 m (5 ft)*
SPREAD *30 m (98 ft)*

ABOVE *Maturing fruits hang in a little cluster amid the characteristically fan-shaped leaves.*

LEFT *A massive ginkgo, decked in its brief golden finery, stands in a Strasbourg park, awaiting the onset of winter.*

RUBBER TREE

Hevea brasiliensis

Many of the trees in this book are included for their pretty flowers, majestic proportions or elegant looks, but this one is here for its beauty of use. Belonging to the family of Euphorbias, all of which secrete a milky sap or white latex, the species is native to the Amazon basin in Brazil. But the rubber tree is now cultivated in far-distant places and is the source of many products in everyday use, from car tyres and tennis balls to washing-up gloves and wetsuits.

Generally best suited to life in lowland tropical forests up to altitudes of 400 metres (1,312 ft) and regularly drenched with rain, the rubber tree is a fast-growing species and in the wild can reach heights of more than 40 metres (131 ft), living for about 100 years. In cultivation, however, it tends to remain smaller, limited to around 25 metres (82 ft) because much of its growing energy is diverted into latex renewal. Plantation trees are generally felled after 25 or 30 years when the latex yield diminishes. Early in the 20th century its natural populations in South America were severely reduced through blight, and plantation efforts in South America have rarely proved successful. Most rubber-tree cultivation in fact now takes place in southeast Asia, effectively begun in 1877 after the Royal Botanic Gardens at Kew, London, sent a consignment of 22 seedlings to the Botanic Gardens in Singapore.

The tree grows with a straight, smooth trunk on which the first branches do not emerge for 10 metres (33 ft) or so, after which the canopy spreads broadly. The bark is decorated with hoop marks. The vessels of the latex-producing system, the phloem, spiral up the tree just beneath its surface so that, when a bark sliver is removed, the latex flows out and can be collected, or 'tapped', into buckets. Generally, trees are not tapped for rubber much before reaching six years of age.

Leaves are palmate, each made up of three small, oval-pointed leaflets. Male and female flowers are small and pale green-white in colour, produced in the axils of the leaves in multiples or panicles rather like the flower heads of hydrangea. Both sexes are contained in the same flower head, with the ephemeral male flowers opening first and lasting for about a day before the females emerge. Pollination is by insects and the resulting fruits are capsules, each of which develops for about six to eight months before releasing its seeds when the fruit splits violently into three lobes.

RUBBER TREE

Deciduous

NATIVE TO *Amazonian rainforest, South America*
HEIGHT *40 m (131 ft)*
TRUNK DIAMETER *0.5 m (2 ft)*
TRUNK GIRTH *1.6 m (5 ft)*
SPREAD *40 m (131 ft)*

ABOVE *Latex is tapped and drained into a bucket after a sliver of bark has been removed from the trunk of the tree.*

LEFT *At an age generally not seen in plantations, this ancient specimen, perhaps a hundred years old, shows off its massive girth in The Company's Gardens, Cape Town.*

MOUNTAIN LACEBARK

Hoheria lyallii

Also called mountain ribbonwoods, two closely related species of this pretty flowering tree belonging to the mallow family thrive on mountainsides in New Zealand's Southern Alps. The genus *Hoheria*, known as lacebarks because of a fibrous lacy mat that runs just beneath the outer layer of bark, includes a total of five species. It is native exclusively to the South Island of New Zealand, not found growing naturally in the wild anywhere else in the world.

Unusually when compared with the rest of New Zealand's native flora, the lacebarks and mountain lacebarks that make up the genus are truly deciduous, shedding their leaves in winter. Mountain lacebarks are small, graceful trees, fast growing but rarely beyond a height of 3 metres (10 ft) so they may be more correctly thought of as shrubs, although their lowland relatives often grow to twice this height. *Hoheria lyallii* typically finds its niche along the scrubby edges of alpine streams and at the margins of denser forests, preferring life on drier, subalpine slopes and rarely climbing beyond 1,000 metres (3,281 ft) in altitude. It often takes root in the paths of old landslips and can regenerate very quckly. Its closest relative, *Hoheria glabrata*, tends to prefer a wetter climate and so grows on the western side of the Alps, which earns more rainfall, while *Hoheria lyallii* congregates more on the eastern slopes. The two species tend to rub shoulders in central Otago. Cultivars are now widely grown in gardens on both North and South Islands.

The soft, downy leaves of the tree change in their appearance as the plant matures. Leaves on a sapling grow narrowly ovate and toothed, fairly sparse and borne on very slender branches, while those clothing the mature plant are broader in profile and about twice the length of the juveniles. There is some argument that this morphological change was a natural adaptation that evolved in the distant past to deter browsing by moas, the large flightless birds of New Zealand since hunted to extinction.

Being hardy, cultivars of mountain lacebark have also become popular with European horticulturalists and can regularly be found on sale in garden centres. The lacebark flowers erupt in midsummer, when the slender boughs can become weighed down with great clusters of sweetly scented, white blossoms not unlike those of a cherry tree in appearance and arising from the axils of the leaves. The fruits of mountain lacebarks are little wingless nuts that readily distinguish them from the winged fruits of the lowland species.

MOUNTAIN LACEBARK

Deciduous

NATIVE TO *New Zealand*
HEIGHT *6 m (20 ft)*
TRUNK DIAMETER *0.3 m (1 ft)*
TRUNK GIRTH *0.9 m (3 ft)*
SPREAD *6 m (20 ft)*

ABOVE *A small tree, barely more than 3 metres (10 ft) tall, growing here on a subalpine slope, clinging to a mountain streamside.*

LEFT *The delicate blooms of the mountain lacebark make a pretty spectacle during the midsummer months on a hillside on New Zealand's South Island.*

HOLLY

Ilex aquifolium

The holly vies with the robin in conjuring up the sweetest images of short, chilly winter days, blazing log fires and the spirit of Christmas. Its feast of brilliant red berries and glossy, vibrant foliage brighten up the countryside when so much else in nature has taken on tones of shrivelled grey and brown and seems to have fallen into a deep sleep.

Holly may often appear to be a small tree or shrub and frequently is present as a manicured hedgerow bush, but left to its own devices and unrestricted by other vegetation, its grey trunk can reach a height of 20 metres (66 ft) at maturity. Aside from a dislike of having its feet in water, it is a hardy tree that will tolerate most conditions and hollies can be found at altitudes of up to 600 metres (1,969 ft). One of the few native broadleaved evergreens occuring in the British Isles, the holly is slow growing and tends to congregate in groves at the edges of forests or where timber has been felled and cleared. It can also occur in dense clumps as part of the woodland understorey. A holly tree can achieve considerable age, but generally does not live much beyond 100 years.

Aside from its brilliant red berries, the tree is best remembered for its glossy leaves, which are prickly and leathery. Each leaf lasts on the tree for about five years before shedding and can arise in two forms. On the lower branches and on younger trees, the leaf bears about five sharp, pointed lobes down each side, while on higher branches and in older trees it grows with a more regular ovate outline and bears only one prickle at the tip. The uncompromising nature of the foliage provides safe shelter for birds, since it tends to deter would-be predators.

Flowers are small and white, each with four petals. They are borne in the axils of the leaves, emerging in late spring and pollinated by bees. The fertilized female flowers give rise to scarlet berries in late autumn, providing Christmas cheer for us and a sumptuous feast for the hungry bird population. The fruits are quite hard but tend to soften after being exposed to the first frosts.

In geological terms, the tree has very ancient origins. It formed a dominant part of the so called laurel forests that clothed much of the Earth some 20 million years ago during the Tertiary period. Today, it tends to be a pioneer species that enriches the soil and paves the way for colonization by other trees.

HOLLY

Evergreen

NATIVE TO *Europe*
HEIGHT *20 m (66 ft)*
TRUNK DIAMETER *0.5 m (2 ft)*
TRUNK GIRTH *1.6 m (5 ft)*
SPREAD *20m (66 ft)*

ABOVE *The bright, glossy red berries of holly bring some welcome cheer to an otherwise chilly and dull winter countryside.*

LEFT *A holly bush, bent and stunted from the work of unforgiving elements, stands exposed on a hillside in the Quantocks, Somerset, England.*

BLUE JACARANDA

Jacaranda mimosifolia

Known to most people simply as jacaranda, this superb flowering tree, with feathery leaves reminiscent of those of mimosa, originates from the tropical and subtropical regions of South America. However, it is now grown as an ornamental in many parts of the world where there is no serious risk of frost, on account of the sheer beauty of its profuse and long-lasting blossoms that breathe the spirit of hot sunny climes and balmy breezes.

The common name of the plant should correctly be pronounced 'zacaranda', in the Portuguese style of pronouncing the letter 'J'. A smallish deciduous tree or shrub growing to no more than 20 metres (66 ft) in height, generally less, it bears spreading branches arising from a short, often disfigured trunk with grey-brown, smooth or slightly scaly bark, and large, feathery pinnate leaves reminiscent of those on a fern.

Blue jacaranda is most commonly seen growing wild across highland slopes up to altitudes of 2,400 metres (7,874 ft), on well-drained sandy soils enjoying goodly amounts of average rainfall. It is one of about 50 related species whose natural range is confined to Central and South America and islands of the West Indies, but which is now found in cultivation all around warmer climes, from the southern United States to the Mediterranean, Africa, India and the Far East. In Australia, the town of Grafton in New South Wales has become famous for its jacarandas, while in South Africa, the city of Pretoria has earned the popular title of 'Jacaranda City'. The trees are able to tolerate short periods of mild frost without permanent damage, but generally need warmth.

In the South American spring and early summer before the leaves unfold, the trees erupt into great branching clusters of flowers, botanically known as panicles, that can be up to 30 centimetres (12 in) deep, consisting of large numbers of deep violet-blue, bell-shaped blooms that are tightly packed together. Each of these individuals consists of five unequal petals joining as a long corolla tube not unlike that of foxglove, and mounted on a red-brown stalk. The flowering period is unusually long, with blossoms appearing on the tree in waves for up to two months. Jacarandas can, however, be temperamental even in the tropics, and may be inclined to poor flowering if the conditions are not quite to their liking.

The seedpods or capsules that follow fertilization, though in nothing approaching the same numbers as the flowers, are woody in nature, each about 5–7 centimetres (2–3 in) across and containing large numbers of flat, winged seeds that are released when the pods split open, generally while still hanging on the branches.

BLUE JACARANDA

Deciduous

NATIVE TO *South America*
HEIGHT *20 m (66 ft)*
TRUNK DIAMETER *0.4 m (1 ft)*
TRUNK GIRTH *1.25 m (4 ft)*
SPREAD *15 m (49 ft)*

ABOVE *The blooms form large, tightly packed clusters or panicles at the tips of the bare branches.*

LEFT *The exquisite violet blossoms of the blue jacaranda smother its branches and make an eye-catching spectacle just before the leaves unfold.*

COMMON WALNUT

Juglans regia

Native to mountains in central Asia, this handsome tree was probably spread through regions of their Empire by the Romans, who grew it for its much-prized edible nuts. In old Anglo-Saxon the word 'walnut' means 'foreign nut', which suggests that from as early as the 5th century there was an awareness in England that the tree was an import either from Gaul or Italy. The title 'common walnut' is probably peculiar to Britain: in America the tree is referred to as the English walnut, and in Australia as the Persian walnut.

A large deciduous tree with a comparatively short trunk clothed in smooth, grey bark and branching into a broad, elegant crown, the walnut can ascend to a height of 35 metres (115 ft) and when fully mature may develop a girth around its trunk base of more than 6 metres (20 ft). It prefers life in full sun and, so long as its roots are provided with good drainage, will tolerate a wide range of soil types. The leaves are pinnate with smooth margins. However the leaflets do not form in opposites but in alternate pairs, with the further addition of a single terminal leaflet. In late springtime the male flowers develop as pendulous catkins each about 10 centimetres (4 in) long, while the tiny green female flowers arise in small erect clusters; although borne on the same tree they mature at different times, thus preventing self-pollination. Once fertilized they mature, by autumn, into oval fruits with a glossy, green outer husk and a woody inner corrugated nutshell housing the large, fleshy seed with its distinctive brain-like folds and ridges.

Walnut trees in general live for not less than 150 years, but as a species there appears to be little information collected about the longevity of *Juglans regia* compared with the American black walnut, *Juglans nigra*. The UK Forestry Commission offers no data for walnut trees grown in parkland beyond 50–55 years.

These days *Juglans regia*, which is moderately frost tolerant, is grown throughout Europe and North America as much for its ornamental appeal as for its culinary value. The tree can be found in the wild at altitudes up to 3,000 metres (9,843 ft). Its original native range extends from western China through the central Asian countries, the Himalayan foothills, and as far west as eastern Turkey. The tree appears to have been introduced to Greece by Alexander the Great in the 4th century BCE, after which its range was further extended through southern Europe by the Roman Empire-builders and it is now cultivated in most temperate regions of the world.

COMMON WALNUT

Deciduous

NATIVE TO *Central Asia*
HEIGHT *35 m (115 ft)*
TRUNK DIAMETER *2 m (7 ft)*
TRUNK GIRTH *6.25 m (21 ft)*
SPREAD *33 m (108 ft)*

ABOVE *The familiar walnut with its wrinkled, brain-like seed, matures on the tree in the safety of a fleshy green outer coat.*

LEFT *The common walnut bears pretty foliage not unlike that of a maple in outline, contrasting here with a tangle of contorted grey branches.*

AFRICAN MAHOGANY

Khaya senegalensis

Native to the African continent and famed less for its natural appearance than for the beauty and durability of its wood, the common name African mahogany distinguishes it from its South American counterpart, which is an altogether different species of tree, though with similar deeply coloured timber. Growing in their native state in tropical forests with high rainfall, and less frequently in open, humid savannahs, mahogany trees were also much planted as ornamentals along urban streets during the African colonial era.

These are mighty trees with rounded, fairly compact profiles, occasionally reaching heights of 45 metres (148 ft) and generally rubbing shoulders tightly with other rainforest trees, but sometimes standing alone in grassy landscapes. They can cope with poor soil conditions and will thrive at altitudes up to 1,800 metres (5,906 ft) so long as there is adequate rainfall. The branches, generally emerging some 10 metres (33 ft) up the trunk, are densely clothed in shiny, evergreen pinnate leaves with between four and six pairs of broadly oval leaflets from which a terminal leaflet is absent. The flowers appear at the start of the rainy season in loose clusters that are small but pretty, each equipped with five yellowish petals and bunches of stamens. Insect pollinated, the fertilized ovary develops into a rounded capsule-like fruit divided into five cells, each containing about six small winged seeds that are released through valves when ripe. The fruits generally remain on the tree through the dry season and the seeds are dispersed by wind. African mahogany tends not to bear fruit for the first 20–25 years of growth.

With its future now severely threatened in some parts of Africa, notably Uganda and Benin, and with little known of its status in other areas, the International Union for the Conservation of Nature now classifies the African mahogany as vulnerable. Despite greater international awareness of the importance of preserving rainforests, it is still subject to excessive exploitation for its wood, and in many areas of Africa reliant on timber production for income, mahogany logging is virtually uncontrolled. It is now, however, cultivated as an ornamental as far distant from Africa as Australia and other parts of southeast Asia.

The tree grows chiefly in what are known ecologically as wet gallery forests. These are areas of dense, evergreen woodland with high rainfall that border river valleys and thin out into the encompassing grassland savannahs. Gallery forests tend, by their damp nature, to be protected from the worst ravages of fires that periodically sweep through drier areas such as savannahs, where most of the rainfall is confined to a short season.

AFRICAN MAHOGANY

Evergreen

NATIVE TO *Africa*
HEIGHT *45 m (148 ft)*
TRUNK DIAMETER *1.2 m (4 ft)*
TRUNK GIRTH *3.75 m (12 ft)*
SPREAD *35 m (115 ft)*

ABOVE *Mahogany matures in thick woods, but through over-logging the oldest examples can now often be found in towns, like this ancient mahogany in Bismarck, South Africa.*

LEFT *Due to the beauty of its wood, the over-exploited African mahogany is fast becoming a rare sight in the shrinking Congo rainforests.*

LABURNUM

Laburnum anagyroides

Probably equally well known to most gardeners as 'gold rain' because of the glorious yellow-gold tresses of flowers that cascade from every branch in early summer, laburnum is highly popular with horticulturalists, but it also has its darker character. Every part of the plant is highly poisonous, including the seeds which, unfortunately, look too much like green peas in their pods to the eyes of small children and can prove dangerous if eaten.

From a distance in late spring, this small Machiavellian tree can take on the appearance of a solid mass of gold. Not growing to any great size, at most 6 metres (20 ft) in height, the laburnum became popular as a garden shrub during the Elizabethan era. A deciduous member of the pea family, it grows at a fast rate. Its smooth-barked trunk tends to be quite short before it expands into large numbers of spreading branches decked with long-stalked trifoliate leaves not dissimilar to those of clover. The tree will tolerate most soil conditions but objects to salt contamination.

The inflorescence of laburnum is, however, its annual star attraction. In the mid-19th century, the original common laburnum was hybridized with another species, Voss's laburnum. The resulting hybrid is the one most commonly found in cultivation today, combining densely packed flower heads with long racemes up to 25 centimetres (10 in) long, and this has given the tree another popular name, 'golden chains'. In May and June the fragrant individual flowers open, each containing both male and female parts arranged much like those of a pea. Pollination is undertaken by insects and after fertilization the female ovary matures into a long pea pod containing the seeds. It is their similarity to edible garden peas that presents the greatest risk for young children, because all parts of the tree synthesize a toxic akaloid called cytisine. Eating sufficient quantity of the seeds can result in vomiting, convulsions and coma. However, although in the UK there are a large number of hospital admissions each year after children have eaten the peas, there appear to be no reported deaths to date as a result of these experiments.

Laburnum wood is not only very hard and durable but also develops contrasting close-grained colours, the heartwood becoming dark chocolate brown while the outer sapwood is a rich yellow. Before artificial wood-staining techniques were developed, these colourful assets earned the timber a high value in the production of veneers. Today, its main use is in cottage-industry wood turning, providing the raw material for anything from decorative bowls to chess pieces.

LABURNUM

Deciduous

NATIVE TO *Southern Europe*
HEIGHT *6 m (20 ft)*
TRUNK DIAMETER *0.3 m (1 ft)*
TRUNK GIRTH *0.95 m (3 ft)*
SPREAD *6 m (20 ft)*

ABOVE *The poisonous laburnum fruit bears an alarming resemblance to an edible pea pod when young, before it ripens and splits into brown valves to release its seeds.*

LEFT *Lethally poisonous in all its parts, the laburnum displays deceptively alluring golden flowers that hang in chains from the branches.*

EUROPEAN LARCH
Larix decidua

The native range of European larch lies in two contrasting areas: the mountainous regions of central Europe and the lowlands of northern Poland. This gives rise to distinct subspecies that produce slightly different cones, the Alpine larch and the Polish larch. The delicate foliage of the larch belies its durability. The tree is able to survive periods of intense cold, its range extending up to 2,400 metres (7,874 ft) in altitude, and in Russia it grows to the limits of the northern tree line, close to the Arctic Circle.

The planting of the tree first became fashionable in the 17th century through the enterprise of John Tradescant, a Kent-born botanist who was head gardener to Charles I. A combination of fast-growing style, durable timber and pretty autumn foliage nowadays makes this tree a favourite of foresters and horticulturalists alike. The forestry use was not always in vogue: in Perthshire, Scotland, for example, for a hundred years it was regarded strictly as an ornamental until the Dukes of Atholl realized the commercial potential and over the next hundred years planted millions of larches across vast swathes of countryside.

Today larch plantation makes up the chief component of many of the man-made forests of Scotland. The tree can grow to considerable height, occasionally reaching 55 metres (180 ft), borne up on a long, rather spindly trunk. In plantations it remains fairly narrow and conical in profile, but left unencumbered by neighbouring trees it can become broad at maturity, with its main limbs reaching out on a level or slightly upward, and the secondary branches drooping down attractively. This offers a cold-climate advantage in that winter snow deposits tend to slip off the tree before building to any depth. The needles emerge in springtime in little dense pom-poms of bright green and expand out into miniature fans, arranged in spirals on the young stems. The needles fall in autumn, leaving the shoots bare but lined with the dormant leaf buds of the following season.

Male flowers take the form of small, yellow catkins that produce vast amounts of pollen, which is transferred on the wind to the bright red, egg-shaped female inflorescences. These mature into green, then brown and woody cones whose winged seeds may subsequently take several years to ripen, be released and blown away.

Worldwide there are 15 species of larch, separated into Old World and New World species. The European larch is not to be confused with the closely related Japanese larch, *Larix kaempferi*, which is often grown as a plantation tree in various parts of Europe and is currently under increasing threat from a fungal pathogen, *Phytophthora ramorum*.

EUROPEAN LARCH

Deciduous

NATIVE TO *Europe*
HEIGHT *55 m (180 ft)*
TRUNK DIAMETER *2 m (7 ft)*
TRUNK GIRTH *6.25 m (21 ft)*
SPREAD *20 m (66 ft)*

ABOVE *The female cones are at first bright red and closed before fertilization, after which they remain ripening on the branches for several years.*

LEFT *One of the few species of conifer that shed their needles in winter, bare European larches clothe a hillside in England's Lake District National Park.*

CAMPBELL'S MAGNOLIA
Magnolia campbellii

In 1855, a year when the great Suffolk-born botanist Joseph Hooker was exploring the foothills of the Himayalas in Sikkim, searching for exotic and undiscovered flora to send back to England, his journey was facilitated by the British government agent in Darjeeling, Archibald Campbell. This tree, now regarded as the finest of all the magnolia species and described by Hooker as being 'so conspicuous a feature of the scenery and vegetation', was named in honour of Campbell's services.

A deciduous tree that grows to 30 metres (99 ft) or more in the wild, Campbell's magnolia is one of over 200 species of a genus whose ancestors, according to fossil remains, date back 20 million years. Magnolia was originally named after the French botanist Pierre Magnol, who was born in 1638 and stands as one of the great innovators of modern plant classification. This species, also known popularly as the 'pink tulip tree', rises above the rest for the sheer size and waxy, exotic beauty of its flowers.

The natural range of the species lies in temperate rainforests extending through sheltered Himalayan valleys up to altitudes of 3,000 metres (9,843 ft), from northern India to southwest China, but also south as far as Myanmar (Burma). It is not particularly frost hardy, but it is now grown as an ornamental in many of the milder temperate climates of the world, including the southwest of the British Isles, where it appears in two closely separated varieties.

The trunk and spreading limbs, clothed with smooth grey bark, bear large and rather thick elliptical, sharp-pointed leaves up to 30 centimetres (12 in) long, but before these unfold in springtime, the flowers produce spectacular displays on the bare branches. It can take up to 30 years for a magnolia to blossom, but when this flowering stage of maturity is finally reached the display of blooms that erupt in their hundreds is worth waiting for. As someone once said, 'the flowers of Campbell's magnolia can only induce one to scurry, wallet in hand, to the local nursery.'

Each flower can be as large as 20 centimetres (8 in) across, varying in colour from white to pastel pink and occasionally crimson. The flower, however, does not conform to a typical floral arrangement, with outer whorls of both petals and sepals. Instead, it consists of a single whorl known as tepals, which effectively combine the role of petal and protective sepal in a type of construction that can also be seen in lilies and tulips. The inner parts of the flower are more conventional, both male and female together, and pollination is mainly facilitated by beetles.

CAMPBELL'S MAGNOLIA

Deciduous

NATIVE TO *The Himalayan range*
HEIGHT *30 m (99 ft)*
TRUNK DIAMETER *0.8 m (3 ft)*
TRUNK GIRTH *2.5 m (8 ft)*
SPREAD *20 m (66 ft)*

ABOVE *The developing inflorescence is protected in bud, not by more typical sepals but by furry green bracts.*

LEFT *Glorious heavy pink blooms, as yet unshrouded by foliage, weigh down the bare branches of Campbell's magnolia in an English arboretum.*

APPLE

Malus domestica

The old saying goes, 'An apple a day keeps the doctor away', and although this may be a rather optimistic forecast, apples do contain healthy quantities of vitamin C. Apples are not only the most recognizable fruits around the globe, but also the most widely cultivated, and today there are more than 7,500 varieties of apple worldwide, all produced from a single ancestor that is still to be found growing wild in parts of western Asia.

The apple is a comparatively small, deciduous tree that bears exquisitely beautiful flowers in spring, followed by profuse quantities of edible fruits in autumn. Its native range stretches through parts of Asia from the republic of Kazakhstan as far as western China, and it contributes significantly to the economies of these countries, to the extent that the capital of Kazakhstan was formerly called Alma Ata, which translates as 'full of apples'. However, the apple is cultivated more or less everywhere in the north temperate zone, from the USA to Japan, and today we produce an annual total of about 60 million tonnes of apples worldwide.

The tree rarely grows beyond a height of 10 metres (33 ft), in a fairly rounded if uneven profile. It is deciduous and in spring bears ovate, dark green leaves with serrated edges and sharp points. At more or less the same time, between April and June, the blossoms unfold in copious masses, beautifully scented, coloured white with a delicate hint of pink. The flowers are monoecious, meaning that both male and female parts are arranged together, and they are insect pollinated. The fruit resulting from fertilization is known in botanical terms as a pome, where the seed-bearing parts of the ovary, the carpels, become surrounded by a fleshy outer layer created from a much-enlarged receptacle, the original 'base' of the flower. Apples begin to ripen in August and, as the leaves start to fall in October, develop a remarkable sweet fragrance of their own.

The orchard apple tree, wherever it is found regardless of commercial variety, originates from one ancient species, *Malus sieversii*. In distant history there is evidence of apples being cultivated from about 7,000 BCE, and probably earlier in the fertile crescent of Mesopotamia (now part of modern Iraq), but it may be more of an apocryphal notion that Eve succumbed to the temptation of apple-scrumping in the Garden of Eden. Apple trees were probably introduced into Britain by the Romans, and the first successful apple orchards were exported to North America from about the mid-17th century.

APPLE

Deciduous

NATIVE TO *Western Asia*
HEIGHT *10 m (33 ft)*
TRUNK DIAMETER *0.5 m (2 ft)*
TRUNK GIRTH *1.6 m (5 ft)*
SPREAD *9 m (30 ft)*

ABOVE *Pastel blossoms unfold in copious sprays from young branches, their heady scent ready to lure in passing insect pollinators.*

LEFT *The broad spread of a solitary apple tree displays all its finery and shades a summer meadow.*

MANGO

Mangifera indica

The mango is the largest fruit tree in the world and produces one of the most delicious of all edible fruits, yet as little as 30 years ago most Europeans had little idea of what a fresh mango looked like, much less of its taste. Times have changed, with economical air cargo rates allowing for the expansion of movement in many more perishable goods from the tropics, and such delicacies are now commonplace in our supermarkets.

The mango is native to the Indian subcontinent and parts of southeast Asia, including most notably Myanmar (Burma), although it is now grown in cultivation throughout the tropical and subtropical regions of the globe. It can mature into a large tree and generally adopts one of two forms. The outline is more often oval, ascending to as much as 40 metres (131 ft) and borne up on a straight, grey trunk with an evenly rounded crown spanning at least 10 metres (33 ft). But the tree can also grow into a broad-spreading habit, the girth occasionally almost matching the height. It develops a very long tap root penetrating 20 metres (66 ft) into the soil, supported by large numbers of widely spreading secondary roots that develop further anchoring systems. Mango can achieve considerable longevity, and some specimen trees are still fruiting after 300 years.

The tree is almost but not entirely evergreen. Rather than shedding and replacing its foliage *en masse*, new leaves appear periodically on selected branches, replacing old, worn-out foliage. Each leaf is large and simple in outline, not unlike that of a laurel, but coloured yellow, orange or pink at first, before turning dark glossy green at maturity, with a broad pale midrib and prominent lateral veins. The tree blossoms in spectacular fashion with masses of small pale flowers, each with five petals, borne in slender upright clusters botanically known as panicles; these showy inflorescences can be as much as 40 centimetres (16 in) tall. A mango tree tends not to produce fruit, however, until it is about six or seven years of age.

The fruit that results from fertilization takes six months to ripen and can then be variable in appearance, from nearly rounded to oblong and sometimes even kidney shaped. The size of individual fruits can also vary considerably, from a few hundred grams to more than 2 kilograms (4 lbs). Each is protected by a smooth, waxy but leathery skin that comes in an array of colours from green to orange, pink or sometimes dark red. The flesh is orange-yellow, reminiscent of peach but more fibrous, and surrounds a large, flat, oblong 'stone'.

MANGO

Deciduous (briefly)

NATIVE TO *India, southeast Asia*
HEIGHT *40 m (131 ft)*
TRUNK DIAMETER *1 m (3 ft)*
TRUNK GIRTH *3 m (10 ft)*
SPREAD *35 m (115 ft)*

ABOVE *The mango ripens in a variety of shapes and sizes at the end of a long, pendulous stalk.*

LEFT *As fruit trees go, the mango is among the tallest, as this fine specimen at Kerala in India reveals.*

NUTMEG

Myristica fragrans

Most of us will be familiar with nutmeg spice residing indispensibly in its jar in the kitchen cupboard, but the evergreen subtropical tree from which the nutmeg comes is probably much less well known. It is a native of the appropriately named Spice Islands of Indonesia, and grows naturally in only one small volcanic cluster of the Moluccas, the Banda Islands, lying some 1,243 miles (2,000 km) east of Java.

I n past centuries nutmeg was a highly prized and fought-over material, not only as a spice for flavouring and preserving frequently less-than-fresh fare, but also as a quack remedy against the plague. It was a sufficiently valuable commodity that Arab traders during the Middle Ages perennially declined to divulge its source, and in the 17th century the Dutch colonial empire waged a particularly vicious local war in order to control nutmeg production, preventing the export of plants from their territory. It was not until the mid-19th century that nutmeg cultivation was finally extended beyond the Banda Islands, and nutmeg trees are now cultivated in Malaysia, parts of southern India, and the island of Grenada in the Caribbean. The trees are separately male and female. Since only the female tree is of any commercial value, with no effective way of sexing the seeds of young trees, growing from seed has proved uneconomic, so the preferred means of propagation is generally by vegetative grafting.

Nutmeg is a fairly small evergreen growing to little more than 20 metres (66 ft) in height, living for between 60 and 80 years, with a bushy rounded outline and otherwise unremarkable appearance. It bears glossy leaves spirally arranged on the stems, ovate in shape with pointed tips, and the inconspicuous yellow flowers are borne in sparse clusters arising from the leaf axils.

The female tree does not produce fruit for at least eight years, reaching a peak of nutmeg production in about 20 years, and the fruit then becomes a source of two distinct spices – nutmeg and mace. The fruit is a rounded drupe about the size of an orange, with white flesh that contains the nutmeg seed. This is clothed with bright red, lacy netting, technically known as an aril, and it is the material of the aril that provides the mace spice. When ripe, the fruit opens, splitting into two valves looking similar to a non-spiny horse chestnut. Today world production of nutmeg amounts to about 12,000 tonnes and that of mace to about 1,500 tonnes, mainly exported from Indonesia and Grenada.

NUTMEG

Evergreen

NATIVE TO *Indonesia*
HEIGHT *20 m (66 ft)*
TRUNK DIAMETER *0.4 m (1 ft)*
TRUNK GIRTH *1.25 m (4 ft)*
SPREAD *20 m (66 ft)*

ABOVE *The nutmeg tree is a fairly small and nondescript evergreen, growing here in a plantation on the Caribbean island of Grenada.*

LEFT *The fruit of the nutmeg yields not one but two much sought-after spices, since the nutmeg seed is clothed with a red aril that is dried to produce mace.*

OLIVE

Olea europaea

The olive tree can hardly claim fame for its beauty, but what it lacks in looks it more than makes up for in other ways, summing up the spirit of the Mediterranean alongside dusty landscapes, vineyards and sparkling blue seas. The olive has been an integral part of our lives since the beginning of recorded history and beyond, and it is one of the plants whose name appears most regularly in the literature of the West.

The native range of the olive extends more or less around the Mediterranean through its European, Asian and north African countries. Demanding a warm, dry and sunny climate in order to thrive at its best, the tree we know today is thought to have been cultivated in antiquity from an original species, *Olea africana*, still found in north Africa, and from there to have been exported widely via ancient Egypt at least 7,000 years ago. A wreath made of olive leaves nearly 3,400 years old was discovered when the sarcophagus of the pharaoh Tutenkhamun was opened, and is now held in the herbarium at Kew Gardens, London. Today it is estimated that more than 750 million olive trees are in cultivation.

Olives are very slow growing, but can also attain a great age and there are unsubstantiated reports of olive trees continuing to produce fruit that are in excess of 1,500 years old. If this is true, they would have first yielded olives well before the birth of the Prophet Muhammad. Belonging to the same family as the ash tree, the olive is a rather squat, bushy evergreen that grows to little more than 15 metres (49 ft) in height with a rounded profile, borne up on a contorted and generally twisted trunk clothed in dark grey bark. The glossy leaves are elliptical in shape with pointed tips, up to 8 centimetres (3 in) long, borne in opposite pairs on the stems and are dark grey-green above, paler on the undersides.

The small, white, feathery-looking flowers, each with four deeply separated petals and two prominent stamens, emerge in clusters or racemes in late spring and in the leaf axils on the twigs of the previous year. The flowers are wind pollinated, and after fertilization the fruit swells into the familiar and much-valued olive. In botanical terms the fruit is a drupe, at first green but becoming progressively darker and blackish-purple as the olive ripens. The stone in the centre is generally referred to as the 'pit'.

In the ancient Greece of Homer, the leafy stems of olive were wound into wreaths and placed upon the brows of winning athletes as the supreme accolade. The olive branch is also a traditional symbol of peace.

OLIVE

Evergreen

NATIVE TO *The Mediterranean*
HEIGHT *15 m (49 ft)*
TRUNK DIAMETER *0.75 m (2 ft)*
TRUNK GIRTH *2.4 m (8 ft)*
SPREAD *15 m (49 ft)*

ABOVE *Olives hang in bunches, ripening to a deep purple under the hot Mediterranean sun.*

LEFT *Ancient gnarled olive trees emerge from the early morning mist in a grove on the Greek island of Thassos.*

COMMON SCREW PINE

Pandanus utilis

Every once in a while plants become popularly mislabelled in a way that points the onlooker in entirely the wrong direction, and trees are no exception. On hearing the name of the common screw pine, one could be forgiven for anticipating visions of a stately conifer restricted to the world's cooler latitudes. In truth, this species can survive only in the tropics, subtropics and the steamy warmth of conservatories, and it bears no relation to a pine tree other than being evergreen.

The so-called 'common' screw pine is frequent only within its restricted native range, and it is one of the very large number of *Pandanus* species, currently believed to include more than 650 members. Limited to the tropical and subtropical regions of the Old World, all are trees and shrubs with palm-like appearance. The natural range of *Pandanus utilis* lies within the Indian Ocean islands of Mauritius, Madagascar and the Seychelles, where it tends to favour life in coastal regions since it is highly tolerant of salt spray carried in the balmy breezes coming off the water. It prefers a place where it has plenty of room to grow without being overshadowed, either in full sun or in a minimum of partial shade. Its unusual rooting system makes it a valuable tree for cultivation on sand dunes, where it plays an important role in binding the sand together and controlling against erosion caused by wind and tides.

The screw pine is, in reality, an evergreen palm tree, growing to a height of no more than 20 metres (66 ft) with a straight trunk that lacks the secondary thickening of tissues found in most other trees. For this reason the trunk cannot support its own weight without the development of large numbers of aerial prop roots, technically known as adventitious roots, that arise from the stem shortly above ground level and fan out, anchoring it into the ground. The top of the trunk bears horizontal branches in tiers creating a pyramid shape, at the ends of which sprout clusters of long, narrow leaves that are twisted on the stems – hence the name 'screw pine'. The leaves are blue-green, with serrated edges made up of sharp, reddish-tinged teeth like a comb, and tapering to a point. The leaves are fibrous, used for thatching and various other commodities, and both trunk and branches are marked with the scars left by old, fallen leaves.

The trees grow as separate male and female plants, and the attractive male flowers are borne in long clusters or racemes. The reference to pine trees comes only from the shape of the fruits, reminiscent of over-sized pine cones or pineapples.

COMMON SCREW PINE

Evergreen

NATIVE TO *Old World tropical and subtropical regions*
HEIGHT *20 m (66 ft)*
TRUNK DIAMETER *0.3 m (1 ft)*
TRUNK GIRTH *0.9 m (3 ft)*
SPREAD *20 m (66 ft)*

ABOVE *The fruit of the screw pine resembles an oversized pine cone and gives rise to its misleading common name.*

LEFT *The slim palm-like leaves of a screw pine standing on the seashore in the Seychelles reveal it as a member of the* Pandanus *palm genus.*

DATE PALM
Phoenix dactylifera

In company with the olive tree, the date palm is not the prettiest of inclusions in this book, but what it lacks in spectacular attributes it makes up for in its priceless practical value. The tree and its sugar-rich fruit have been an indispensible part of life in the Middle East from a time in antiquity long before written history began, and today varieties of date are cultivated worldwide anywhere that climate permits.

Phoenix dactylifera is one of large group of some 2,500 tropical and subtropical trees in the family Arecaceae, generally referred to as palms. Aside from this species, the coconut palm is probably the most familiar. The date palm is a tall evergreen that grows to about 30 metres (98 ft) in height on a single slim trunk, ending in a cluster of radiating, much-divided fronds, thus looking not unlike a feather duster. The trunk is marked from the base upwards in geometric spiralling patterns that are created by the sheaths remaining from the bases of fallen leaves. The foliage takes the form of alternating pinnate fronds up to 6 metres (20 ft) in length, and these remain on the tree for as much as seven years. The higher fronds are upright, while the lower members radiate more downwards. Their individual leaflets are silvery grey-green in colour, leathery and lanceolate with sharp tips that deter would-be grazers.

The trees are dioecious, so male and female flowers are borne on separate plants, and although pollination is by wind action where trees grow in the wild, cultivated date palms are usually pollinated manually. The male plants are of value purely as pollinators, and a single male tree will serve to pollinate 100 females. Individual blooms are small, white and fragrantly scented, arranged in elongated clusters or spikes up to 1 metre (3 ft) in length and arising from the leaf axils.

In botanical terms, the fruit resulting from fertilization is a drupe consisting of a fleshy fibrous pericarp enclosing a single seed. These fruits hang in pendulous clusters and the individual drupe, which is oblong and up to 7 centimetres (3 in) in length, looks rather like a fat finger – hence the origin of the Greek species name *dactylifera*, meaning 'finger like'.

The seed of the date palm possesses extraordinary longevity. After lying dormant for a period known to be in the region of 2,000 years, seed from one of the older cultivars, referred to as the Judean palm and thought to have been extinct, has now been successfully germinated. The seed was unearthed during excavations at the Dead Sea archaeological site of Mount Masada and radio-carbon dated. Having been planted in a pot in 2005, it subsequently sprouted and thus became accepted as the oldest known viable seed.

DATE PALM

Evergreen

NATIVE TO *Old World tropical and subtropical regions*
HEIGHT *30 m (98 ft)*
TRUNK DIAMETER *0.4 m (1 ft)*
TRUNK GIRTH *1.25 m (4 ft)*
SPREAD *10 m (33 ft)*

ABOVE *Each fruit is botanically known as a drupe, and contains a single seed enclosed in a fleshy coat rich in sticky sugar.*

LEFT *Heavy clusters of ripening fruits hang from the leaf axils atop a sturdy trunk and catch the first rays of the morning sun.*

NORWAY SPRUCE

Picea abies

Few people in the West will fail to recognize the Norway spruce as the most popular and oldest traditional Christmas tree. However, the specimens that are cut out of forest nurseries, fixed into pots and decorated with baubles once a year in our living rooms are mere striplings compared with some of the mighty specimens found in the wild. The tallest today is believed to be one standing in the Sutjeska National Park in Bosnia-Herzegovina, estimated to reach 63 metres (207 ft) into the clouds, although the height has not been accurately measured.

The native range of *Picea abies* is not limited to Norway and it is found growing in the wild extensively across Europe, from Scandinavia down to the Balkans and northern Greece. Through large tracts of Russia it has been hybridized with a related species, the Siberian spruce, *Picea obovata*, and it has also been naturalized in some parts of North America. It will grow happily up to altitudes of 1,000 metres (3,281 ft) but is sometimes found at twice this elevation in some areas, including the Bavarian Alps. Specimen trees can live for more than 400 years in the more northerly latitudes, but generally become weakened or diseased after 200 years in North America.

A large evergreen conifer with a narrowly conical crown when young, the outline broadens and becomes more flat topped with age. The fairly short branches are angled slightly upwards, other than at the tips and near the ground where they tend to droop. They are borne on a straight trunk of only moderate girth, clothed with reddish-brown bark. Despite the great height that the tree can attain, the trunk rarely reaches a circumference greater than 1.5 metres (5 ft) around the base. The foliage consists of short, dark green needles with blunt tips that are at first tufted on the end of stems and then become spirally arranged as the stem elongates.

The individual inflorescence is either male or female, borne on the same tree and emerging in May and June. Pollination takes place through wind action, and the cones that result from fertilization are elongated, hanging from the tips of the branches, the scales at first green and then becoming brown. Today, Norway spruce is one of the most frequently planted members of the genus and is of considerable economic importance, not only for seasonal felling as Christmas trees but also as a ready source of timber. Its seeds germinate easily, it grows at a moderate speed for the first 25 years, increasing to a maximum between this and 60 years of age, and it produces good-quality, straight-grained softwood for use in the construction industry, furniture making and in paper manufacture.

NORWAY SPRUCE

Evergreen

NATIVE TO *Europe*
HEIGHT *50 m (164 ft)*
TRUNK DIAMETER *1.5 m (5 ft)*
TRUNK GIRTH *4.7 m (15 ft)*
SPREAD *15 m (49 ft)*

ABOVE *Among the most popular of Christmas trees, Norway spruce is also grown commercially as a source of timber for construction.*

LEFT *Dusted with a fresh coat of snow, ranks of Norway spruce stand braced against the winter frost in the Taunus Forest in Germany.*

LACEBARK PINE

Pinus bungeana

This extraordinarily pretty tree is a native of mountains in northeastern and central China. Its main attraction is not so much the needle-like foliage, in appearance much like that of other pines, but the picturesque nature of its bark. This peels repeatedly away from the multiple trunks to reveal a lacy patchwork of rounded areas that are at first variously coloured before turning silvery white.

First brought to the attention of the West in 1831 by German botanist Alexander von Bunge, who named the lacebark pine when he found it growing in the vicinity of Buddhist temples near Beijing, it was another 15 years before the Scottish plant hunter, Robert Fortune, collected seed and sent it to England. Today, one of the oldest living specimens outside China stands in Kew Gardens, London. Favouring life on limestone slopes with their roots well anchored among rocks, the mature trees can reach 20 metres (66 ft) tall in the wild, although in cultivation they rarely achieve more than 15 metres (49 ft). Although hardy in a temperate climate, the tree tends to be very slow growing, putting on as little as 2 metres (6.5 ft) in the first ten years. It also takes at least this length of time for the bark to begin its characteristic peeling, technically known as exfoliation.

Unlike most other pines that arise on a single trunk, the lacebark pine is multi-stemmed and so may tend to look more like a shrub, at first with a broadly conical outline but then with age becoming more flat topped and almost as wide as it is tall. Only the main horizontal branches grow to any length, and the foliage takes the form of dark green needles, arranged in bundles of three, each with particularly spiky tips. Flowers are small and insignificant, separately male and female, and pollination is by wind. The cones that result from fertilization are light brown in colour and egg shaped, with limited numbers of scales protecting the seeds. These cone scales are also spiny tipped.

Various cultivars are now grown commercially and one of the most sought after is the 'silver ghost' tree, so called because it has been developed to display an eye-catching silvery grey bark. In most other varieties, as in the native species, the bark when first exposed is a multi-coloured blend of white, purple and olive, only becoming pure milk-white as it ages.

The tree has long been popular on account of its patchwork bark for planting in the vicinity of Chinese Buddhist temples. It is also seen extensively in ornamental parks throughout southeast Asia, and in some oriental beliefs it is a tree that symbolizes longevity.

LACEBARK PINE

Evergreen

NATIVE TO *Northeast and central China*
HEIGHT *20 m (66 ft)*
TRUNK DIAMETER *1.1 m (4 ft)*
TRUNK GIRTH *3.4 m (11 ft)*
SPREAD *20 m (66 ft)*

ABOVE *The lacebark pine tends to develop a squat, shrubby appearance because, unlike other conifers, it often grows as a multi-stemmed tree.*

LEFT *The tree earns its popular name because the bark adopts a habit of peeling away in flakes to reveal a multi-coloured patchwork quilt beneath.*

PONDEROSA OR WESTERN YELLOW PINE

Pinus ponderosa

This tree is aptly named, not so much because of its height, which is impressive enough, but on account of the huge mass of timber that it produces. Growing naturally in the Cascade Mountains that run north from California along the western seaboard of North America, it is the tallest of the world's pine species, reaching heights of 72 metres (236 ft) and dwarfing many other trees in the forest.

Native to North America, the species was first discovered growing in a forested area near Washington in 1826 by the plant collector David Douglas, who gives his name to another colossus among conifers, the Douglas fir, and three slightly different subspecies have been recognized based on their geographic distribution. A mature ponderosa pine is a mighty tree by any standards, regularly exceeding 40 metres (131 ft) in height, and it can attain a diameter across the trunk base of up to 2 metres (7 ft) or more. In January 2011 a single huge specimen growing in the Siskiyou National Forest in Oregon was measured using laser apparatus and found to be just short of 82 metres (269 ft) high.

Ponderosa pine, which is also known locally as the western yellow pine, requires free living space around itself and will not readily tolerate the shade of other trees. It can be found forming extensive forests on mountain slopes at altitudes of up to 3,000 metres (9,843 ft) and is thus a common sight on high plateaus. A long-lived species, it can sometimes not reach full maturity for as many as 400 years, growing generally with a fairly narrowly conical outline. When fully mature, however, a veteran tree often displays an open, spreading crown or even a flattened, 'thunderhead' top.

The bark of the trunk and main limbs is quite distinctive. Having started life very dark or almost black, for which reason the immature trees are also known as 'blackjacks', the bark takes on a cinnamon-reddish hue as it ages and the outer layers fracture into plates separated by deep black furrows or crevices. Ponderosa pine is clothed with particularly long yellowish-green evergreen needles, with serrated edges, arranged in bundles of three, occasionally two, that live on the tree for up to six years before being shed.

The male and female cones are borne separately on the same tree, appearing in May and June. The male cones are small, of insignificant appearance and arranged in little clusters. Pollination is through wind action and the female cones, when mature after two years, are about 10 centimetres (4 in) long, the individual scales that protect the developing seeds armed with outwardly directed prickles at their tips. The seeds are winged.

PONDEROSA PINE

Evergreen

NATIVE TO *West coast of North America*
HEIGHT *72 m (236 ft)*
TRUNK DIAMETER *1.2 m (4 ft)*
TRUNK GIRTH *3.75 m (12 ft)*
SPREAD *8 m (26 ft)*

ABOVE *A cluster of male cones, laden with pollen, arise from the branch tips and await the breeze to carry their cargo to the female cones.*

LEFT *This majestic ponderosa pine has been growing towards the meagre sunlight for years in Utah's Bryce Canyon National Park in the United States.*

MONTEREY PINE

Pinus radiata

This beautiful and stately conifer is restricted in its native range, as its popular name Monterey pine suggests, to the coastal region of central California in the United States, where it is now under severe threat for its survival from a fungal pathogen that causes pine pitch canker. Away from California, however, the tree is among the most extensively planted of all pine species worldwide on account of its commercial timber value.

Monterey pine is a species of great antiquity, its ancestors having migrated into California from Central America some 15 million years ago. Sadly, there are no more than three stands still surviving in Monterey County and all are under threat, but elsewhere close to 4,000,000 hectares (9,884,000 acres) of *Pinus radiata* are being grown commercially in plantations, chiefly in Chile and New Zealand. In the wild the trees are not seen reaching much beyond 30 metres (98 ft) in height, but some specimens in cultivation can achieve almost double this size at full maturity. The trees are salt tolerant but will not cope with frosts, and tend not be grown successfully at altitudes higher than 1,000 metres (3,281 ft).

When young the trees are more or less conical and fairly neat in shape, but as they age their appearance can become more open and irregular, with a flattish crown. If they grow on exposed coasts, the winds can sculpt them to look even more dishevelled and ragged. The tree is carried up on a stout, straight trunk as much as 2 metres (7 ft) in diameter, clothed with dark reddish and eventually deeply furrowed bark. Needles are long and slender with blunt tips, bright green and carried in clusters of three.

One of the notable features of the Monterey pine lies in its production of so-called closed cones. This aspect contrasts with most pines, in which the fertilized cone opens and sheds its seed after the first season. The closed habit is botanically known as serotiny, and may be seen as an adaptation in conifers that are regularly exposed to risk from forest fires. The female cone is effectively sealed with resin and remains closed on the tree until at least the second year after fertilization. It may then open and close several times again, depending on prevailing weather conditions. Serotiny is thus thought to be an insurance mechanism to maintain survival of the species. Seed may be stored in the cones until a fire sweeps through an area and the heat melts the resin, and although the parent tree dies its cones then open and release viable seed to recolonize the burnt ground.

MONTEREY PINE

Evergreen

NATIVE TO *California coast, North America*
HEIGHT *30 m (98 ft)*
TRUNK DIAMETER *2 m (7 ft)*
TRUNK GIRTH *3.2 m (10 ft)*
SPREAD *30 m (98 ft)*

ABOVE *Tiny developing female cones arise from the young branch tips, where they may remain for several years before shedding their seeds.*

LEFT *A ghostly army of tall Monterey pine trunks emerges from the morning fog that rolls in regularly from the ocean on the coast of southern California.*

SCOTS PINE

Pinus sylvestris

Although widely recognized as the Scots pine, the name of this evergreen is rather misleading because the native range generally extends from northern Britain across Europe and Asia eastwards into Siberia, as well as down to the more southerly latitudes of Spain and Portugal. However, in the British Isles it now only grows truly wild in Scotland, having been felled to extinction for its timber in England and Wales some 300 years ago before being reintroduced later as a forestry plantation species.

The Scots pine is the only species of evergreen conifer properly native to northern Europe, and it was one of the pioneer trees that colonized the bare ground after the last Ice Age. In Britain, hundreds of years ago, it formed the main element of the ancient Caledonian Forest that covered vast tracts of the Scottish Highlands. Only scattered remnants of that forest still cling on in protected areas, although great swathes of man-made plantation now cover much of the landscape. A similar story of decline and reintroduction has taken place in other parts of the tree's once-natural range. The culprits have been an insatiable demand for timber over the centuries and predation of saplings by grazing stock.

Scots pine will grow to 25 metres (82 ft) in height, occasionally more, and is fairly long lived with specimen trees still standing after 300 years. It can tolerate life at sea level and up to altitudes of 1,000 metres (3,281 ft) in the north of its range, reaching twice that elevation in warmer, more southerly latitudes. Because the species can develop either a deep tap root or spreading shallow roots, it is very adaptable to life in a range of soil types. The tree possesses a fairly open appearance, with twisting, heavy branches that tend to be short, and the very apex of the trunk often has a distorted, wiggly shape. From a distance the mature tree has a broad, rather flatly domed profile that generally looks windblown and ragged, particularly on exposed slopes. The bark of the broad, robust trunk is grey in young trees but becomes a warm reddish-brown and deeply seamed as the tree reaches maturity. The needles on Scots pine are carried in bunches of two and are about twice as long on young specimens as on older, mature trees.

Male and female cones emerge in spring on the same tree, with the females arising higher up than the males, towards the ends of branches, and pollination is by wind. After fertilization the familiar female cones take two years to develop and ripen, and while they are still attached to the branches, the cone scales open to release their cargoes of tiny winged seeds.

SCOTS PINE

Evergreen

NATIVE TO *Europe, northern Asia*
HEIGHT *25 m (82 ft)*
TRUNK DIAMETER *1 m (3 ft)*
TRUNK GIRTH *3.2 m (10 ft)*
SPREAD *22 m (72 ft)*

ABOVE *The male cones of Scots pine arise as 'golden candles' at the tips of young branches a little below their female counterparts.*

LEFT *A Scots pine stands sentinel-like at the edge of Loch an Eilein deep in the Scottish Highlands.*

JAMAICA DOGWOOD

Piscidia piscipula

This is a small tropical species whose native range is more or less restricted to the coastal regions fringing the Caribbean. It bears pretty pastel pink flowers similar in appearance to those of a pea, but the tree also has a sinister side to its nature that is indicated by another of its popular names, the 'Florida fish poison tree'. Indeed, its botanical name *Piscidia* translates as 'killer of fish'.

The tissues of *Piscidia piscipula* generate a powerful narcotic that serves to stun fish when extracts from the tree are thrown into their water, and it is not the only species that is used in this way; an east African tree, *Barringtonia asiatica*, has similar properties. The Caribbean species is also sometimes known as 'fish fuddle' and has been extensively used as both a sedative and an analgesic in local herbal medicine for the treatment of a variety of conditions from migraines to insomnia.

The native range of the Jamaica dogwood extends somewhat beyond the North American state of Florida. It is also found growing in the Bahamas, the Greater Antilles, Mexico and other maritime regions of Central America. The tree is limited to coastal areas and prefers life on well-drained sandy or limestone soils covered with an amount of surface humus. It can cope equally with drought and with limited periods of inundation by brackish or salt water, and can be found associated with mangroves, but it dislikes the direct exposure to salt spray on its foliage and will not tolerate cold conditons.

A comparatively small deciduous species, it grows to a maximum of 15 metres (49 ft) in parts of Florida, with a sturdy trunk clothed in thin, green-grey bark that becomes scaly with darker mottled patches as it ages. The mature tree develops an open, airy profile with stout, upwardly directed but often twisted and distorted branches, and adjacent trees may become tightly packed together. The foliage takes the form of compound leaves, pinnately arranged, each ovate leaflet dark green above, grey-green below, and somewhat downy.

The tree blossoms after four or five years, and the flowers are undoubtedly its prettiest feature. Arranged like those of a pea, they emerge in clusters or panicles in May and are pastel coloured, mainly white tinged with green, but with distinctive pinkish-purple stripes on the keel petals and with a purple flushed calyx of fused sepals that protects the flower in bud. The flowers are insect pollinated, chiefly by bees, and the fruits resulting from fertilization are elongated pods, also like those of a pea or bean, ripening in July and August with four papery wings and containing the reddish-brown seeds.

JAMAICA DOGWOOD

Deciduous

NATIVE TO *Southern North America, Central America*
HEIGHT *15 m (49 ft)*
TRUNK DIAMETER *1 m (3 ft)*
TRUNK GIRTH *3.2 m (10 ft)*
SPREAD *15 m (49 ft)*

ABOVE *The flowers are the tree's prettiest feature, emerging in May in pastel panicles and unfolding to reveal bright pink stripes.*

LEFT *A gnarled specimen tree of Jamaica dogwood with its characteristically distorted tangle of branches, stands at Buck Key, Florida.*

LONDON PLANE

Platanus x acerifolia

An aptly named tree, this is one of the most familiar sights along the leafy streets of London. The London plane is actually a hybridization that resulted from a chance encounter in Spain during the 17th century, when two related species planted close together cross-fertilized with one another. The resulting seed grew into an intermediate form, bridging the features of the parent species.

Because it amounts to a hybridization, which is thought to have taken place in the 1640s, the Latin name of London plane is generally written as *Platanus x acerifolia*. The tree is thus a mixture of the genes of *Platanus orientalis*, the oriental plane, and *Platanus occidentalis*, the American sycamore, with its leaves and flowers displaying some of the characteristics of both parents. The hybrid was first described in 1789 by the Scottish botanist William Aiton, who studied a specimen tree growing at Kew Gardens, London, and named it the Spanish plane tree.

London plane is a deciduous species growing to about 35 metres (115 ft) in height, occasionally rather more, that has been found exceptionally tolerant of the bustle and grime of life overseeing polluted urban streets. Mainly for this reason, it has been planted extensively for centuries in London. From England its popularity then spread across the Atlantic, where it is now an equally common sight on the streets of North American cities from New York to Los Angeles.

The tree grows on a sturdy trunk whose grey-green bark characteristically flakes off, revealing irregular creamy white patches, until it reaches an advanced age when the colour of the bark becomes a browner shade and tends to crack and thicken rather than exfoliate. The limbs are spreading, so the tree can appear almost as wide as it is tall when fully mature, with a rather rounded profile. The foliage, borne alternately on the stems, has between three and five lobes much like that of a sycamore or maple. The young leaves are at first clothed in downy hairs, although these wear off as the season progresses.

The tiny greenish-yellow flowers are borne in clusters on long stems, with male and female inflorescence produced separately, albeit on the same tree. The male flowers, with anything up to eight stamens each, generate copious quantities of pollen in May, which is carried on the wind and is well known for tormenting those allergic to it. The male flowers then fall from the branches. The result of fertilization is the development of masses of little green 'balls' packed with tiny fruits in the form of achenes. The balls disintegrate at maturity, releasing the fruits that are then dispersed on the wind, facilitated by tufts of little hairy attachments.

LONDON PLANE

Deciduous

NATIVE TO *Europe,*
North America
HEIGHT *35 m (115 ft)*
TRUNK DIAMETER *1 m (3 ft)*
TRUNK GIRTH *3.2 m (10 ft)*
SPREAD *32 m (105 ft)*

ABOVE *The plane tree bears leaves that are reminiscent of those of maple or acer, hence its Latin species name,* acerifolia.

LEFT *A veteran London plane tree graces an urban park in all its crooked splendour.*

FRANGIPANI
Plumeria rubra

The exquisitely perfumed blossoms of this tropical tree probably need little introduction. Also known as the 'temple tree', its better-known name is owed to an aristocratic Roman family called Frangipani, literally meaning 'bread-breakers'. One of its members, the Marquese Frangipani, invented a perfume for scenting gloves in the 16th century. When *Plumeria rubra* came to the attention of Europeans, its perfume was thought reminiscent of Marquese Frangipani's invention.

The frangipani tree grows to a height of 8 metres (26 ft) in a spreading, much-branched habit, so it may also be considered a large shrub. Its New World native range includes Mexico, Central and South America as far as Venezuela, and the Caribbean, thus another of its familiar local names is West Indian jasmine. But its enormous popularity as a cultivated ornamental means that it is grown more or less anywhere in the world that mild climate permits. From the more southerly parts of the USA to Hawaii, Sri Lanka and northern Australia, it can be found gracing urban streets, parks and gardens. It is also planted regularly in the grounds of temples. In Hawaii, frangipani is grown commercially on a large scale because the blooms form an essential part of the traditional Hawaiian garland of celebration, the *lei*.

The tree is carried up on a thick, succulent trunk clothed with a grey bark that is thin and readily oozes with a white sap or latex when damaged. The trunk generally branches profusely and the limbs are brittle. The fat, stubby branches tend to grow to a similar length, creating an open, spreading crown, and the tree can thus take on the semblance of an umbrella. The deciduous leaves are large, up to 50 centimetres (20 in) long, and coarsely ovate, but they grow in clusters only at the tips of the branches. They are shed for a fairly short period during the winter months, and the species prefers life in full sun on a well-drained soil.

It is, of course, the flowers for which frangipani is rightly acclaimed, because of their glamorous appearance and intense, delightful fragrance. The flowers also emerge at the tips of the branches, just before the leaves unfurl, in clusters or cymes from June through to November. An individual bloom includes five petals, all slightly twisted against one another so as to resemble a flat spiral. Each separate petal has either a yellow or pinkish base and can then be white or pink tinged, or wholly pink. The most frequently seen shade is pink, from which the Latin species name *rubra* comes. But there is also a popular white and yellow cultivar named 'Singapore' that produces flowers all year round where it is grown commercially in Hawaii.

FRANGIPANI

Deciduous

NATIVE TO *Central and South America*
HEIGHT *8 m (26 ft)*
TRUNK DIAMETER *0.4 m (1 ft)*
TRUNK GIRTH *1.25 m (4 ft)*
SPREAD *8 m (26 ft)*

ABOVE *A frangipani tree in bloom graces ornamental gardens at Funchal on the Portuguese island of Madeira.*

LEFT *The tree takes its name from the Marquese Frangipani's perfume reminiscent of the tree's exotically glamorous flowers.*

TOTARA
Podocarpus totara

In company with Maori war dances, flightless birds and snowy mountain peaks, this tree exudes the spirit of New Zealand. It ranges naturally through both the South and North Islands, from the lowlands to lower mountain slopes. Totara is a big tree whose ancestors have probably been around since the last Ice Age. A relative, *Podocarpus nubigenus,* so close genetically that it is hard to tell the two apart, comes from South America and is a reminder of the Antarctic bridge that once existed between the great land masses of the southern hemisphere.

This is another mighty specimen of an evergreen, reminiscent in some respects of a yew, and the largest member of the Podocarpaceae family. It has long been popular in cultivation in parks on account of its impressive size. Capable of surviving for 500 years, perhaps longer, it grows slowly up to a height of at least 30 metres (98 ft), which is not exceptionally tall, although a veteran tree standing in the Pureora Forest Park is alleged to have reached 51 metres (167 ft) tall. But the limbs are borne on what eventually becomes a ponderously massive trunk, which can be up to 3 metres (10 ft) in diameter, spreading at its base with equally enormous roots that quest outwards, serpent like, over the surface of the forest floor.

The bark is thick, fibrous and deeply furrowed, reddish-brown at first and becoming progressively greyer before it is shed in long, cork-like strips. The foliage is densely packed and takes the form of dull, bronze-green needles that are erect, leathery and sharp tipped. In veteran specimens the appearance becomes more open and the upper branches tend to die off, leaving a somewhat ragged and gaunt appearance against the skyline.

Male and female cones are borne on different trees and are pollinated by the wind. The female false 'fruit' that results from fertilization is a fleshy, swollen, red receptacle, not unlike a yew aril, but unlike the fruit of the yew, the seed is borne perched on the end of the fleshy part, rounded in shape and covered by a tough, green outer coat.

The timber of totara is immensely hard, straight grained and highly resistant to decay. It has been the favoured material used in the crafting of the massive Maori war canoes, and for much of their traditional carving and sculpture. The Maori regard totara as a sacred tree, one of the children of the god of forests, Tane, and it is now subject to strict felling restriction in the wild.

TOTARA

Evergreen

NATIVE TO *New Zealand*
HEIGHT *30 m (98 ft)*
TRUNK DIAMETER *3.5 m (11 ft)*
TRUNK GIRTH *11 m (36 ft)*
SPREAD *20 m (66 ft)*

ABOVE *The totara is a coniferous evergreen that bears densely packed, leathery needles.*

LEFT *The deeply furrowed trunk of an 1,800-year-old totara resolutely defies the advancing years in New Zealand's Pureora Forest Park.*

WHITE POPLAR

Populus alba

White poplar, also commonly known as abele, is a tree that grows fast, has a short lifespan and is much admired for its white bark and aspen-like leaves, with their very pale white-grey under-surfaces. With a more rounded profile than aspen, it also tends to be more geographically distinct in a native range that extends through central and southern Europe, dipping into western Asia but going little further.

Closely related to aspen, and sometimes hybridizing with it into the grey poplar, so called on account of the downy grey coating of its foliage, the white poplar grows to much the same height, possibly a little taller, reaching 25 metres (82 ft) at most. Its appearance, however, tends to be broader, with a thicker trunk and a more rounded crown, although the tree can develop an unevenly ragged outline as it matures. Its preferred accommodation is on moist ground where it often fringes riversides and lakes. Although its true native range is moderately restricted, the tree is cultivated extensively in parks and gardens because of its looks. It was introduced into North America in the mid-18th century, where it is now grown as an ornamental in many states on the eastern seaboard. Like the aspen, it is an opportunist tree that will quickly colonize ground where there is not too much competition for space.

The tree is carried up on a straight trunk coated with smooth white bark in young specimens, but it becomes pock-marked with diamond-shaped lenticel scars as it ages. The prettiest feature of the white poplar is undoubtedly its deciduous foliage. The leaves when they first unfurl in spring are covered entirely with white woolly down, but after a week or so they shed most of this protective mantle and become more vividly patterned, glossy dark green on the upper surface with contrasting whitish-grey underneath. In a breeze they tend to turn upside down, creating a dramatic effect of predominantly white colour. The individual leaf is rounded, with shallow maple-like lobes, and the foliage turns gold-coloured in the autumn.

The tree flowers in early spring, with male and female flowers borne on separate trees, and the inflorescence is a catkin pollinated by wind. The dangly male catkins are grey but are brightened with dark red stamens, and their female counterparts are a dull green. The female catkins increase in size after fertilization, and the resultant fruit is a capsule containing tiny wind-blown seeds. In common with the aspen, the white poplar will also readily extend its presence through the production of suckers.

WHITE POPLAR

Deciduous

NATIVE TO *Old World northern hemisphere*
HEIGHT *25 m (82 ft)*
TRUNK DIAMETER *0.8 m (3 ft)*
TRUNK GIRTH *2.5 m (8 ft)*
SPREAD *25 m (82 ft)*

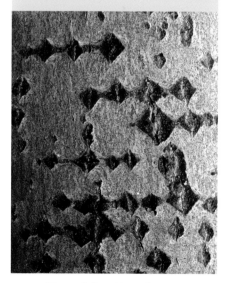

ABOVE *Diamond-shaped lenticel scars characterize the bark of white poplar.*

LEFT *The trunks of densely packed white poplars create a pretty spectacle in spring sunlight.*

ASPEN

Populus tremula

One of the family of poplars and extending across much of Europe and Asia in a very wide range, this is a pretty and graceful tree. It is admired not so much on account of its flowers, which are small and insignificant, but because of its delicate summer clothing of leaves that flutter like frantic butterflies even in the slightest breeze, and make constant rustling noises that are said to sound like a cascading stream.

The European aspen, also known as the 'trembling poplar', occasionally hybridizes with *Populus alba*, the white poplar of central and southern Europe. Its North American counterpart is *Populus tremuloides*, from which it differs only in bearing less coarsely toothed leaves. The aspen qualifies as one of the most widely distributed of all the world's tree species, its natural range extending from south of the Arctic Circle to north Africa, and east as far as Japan.

The mature tree reaches 25 metres (82 ft) in height and is fast growing. It serves as a successful pioneer species, but in the wild it then tends to be short lived since it is eventually crowded out of woodlands by other slower-growing species and dislikes being shaded from the sun. If left uncontested in open areas, it tends to survive for longer. Aspen is essentially a species of lowlands but can be found on mountain slopes up to 1,800 metres (5,906 ft) in more southerly latitudes. It does not grow well, however, on chalk soils.

The straight, slender trunk is clothed in smooth, grey bark pockmarked with dark, diamond-shaped scars of old breathing pores, known as lenticels. The bark becomes darker and more seamed in older trees. The branches angle upwards and overall the tree displays a narrow, open profile with the lower half of the trunk generally left bare of foliage. The unfolding leaves are at first tinted bronze, only becoming fully green after several weeks. Adult leaves are rounded with wavy, toothed edges and their capacity to flutter is explained by an unusual flattening of the leaf stalks or petioles. Leaves on juvenile saplings tend to be triangular in outline, elongated and rather larger than their counterparts on mature trees.

Aspen trees regularly spread themselves vegetatively by means of suckers, and their seed tends not to set in more northerly latitudes. Flowers appear early in the spring before the leaves unfold and form small, greenish, wind-pollinated catkins, male and females borne on separate trees. The catkins are hairy, the males extending to about 10 centimetres (4 in) long, while their female counterparts run to about half that length. After fertilization the fruits mature into little capsules containing minute seeds, each coated in a fluff that allows them to be carried considerable distances on the wind when the ripened capsules split open in early summer.

ASPEN

Deciduous

NATIVE TO *Old World northern hemisphere*
HEIGHT *25 m (82 ft)*
TRUNK DIAMETER *0.8 m (3 ft)*
TRUNK GIRTH *2.5 m (8 ft)*
SPREAD *25 m (82 ft)*

ABOVE *The fruits of the aspen bear little fluffy tails that allow them to be dispersed over considerable distances on the wind.*

LEFT *As summer fades, the golden, changing colours of aspen trees are sharply etched against a dark background of conifers in the mountains of Piedmont, northern Italy.*

The golden leaves of aspens in the North American fall present a dramatic contrast with dark, moody conifers against the snows of Rocky Mountain peaks near Telluride, USA.

CHERRY

Prunus avium

The *Prunus* genus includes several members that will be instantly familiar for their fruits, including plums, cherries, peaches, apricots and almonds. A number of species, including *Prunus avium*, have been cultivated purely as ornamentals whose principal feature is their beautiful blossom, and these generally do not produce good edible fruit. Cherry trees grown specifically for their fruit are generally varieties of *Prunus cerasifera*.

The native range of these species of largely deciduous small trees and shrubs, of which there are more than 400 different kinds, extends right across the northern hemisphere. Cherry trees found growing in the wild generally reach a maximum height of about 15 metres (49 ft), often much less when cultivated in orchards or gardens. The ornamental trees have become a familiar sight on urban roadsides throughout Europe. In Japan the cultivation of flowering varieties is more or less an art form, and the blossom of the cherry is featured in much of traditional Japanese decoration.

All the *Prunus* species bear simple, ovate leaves with serrated edges and pointed tips. One of the more engaging features of many lies in their flowering, which can take place very early in the year. The first signs of blossoms emerging may be in late January or early February when there is snow on the ground.

In *Prunus avium*, also known as the wild cherry or bird cherry, the flowers are delicately formed with five petals and are borne in clusters, botanically called corymbs, of up to six individuals, appearing in March. *Prunus cerasifera* varieties generally flower a month earlier in mid-February. Although the flowers themselves are small, massed together in profusion on the bare branches of a tree before the leaves unfold, they are a glorious sight and a fitting herald of the spring that is to come. A cherry tree in full bloom can look from a distance to be an uninterrupted 'cloud' of white. In the wild forms, the flowers including both the male and female parts are always pure white with yellow stamens, but cultivated varieties may be grown with pastel pink tints to the petals.

The familiar cherry fruit is technically called a drupe, in which the outer part of the fertilized ovary wall becomes fleshy and surrounds a single seed enclosed in a stony inner layer, the endocarp. The fruits ripen from August to September, initially green but then transforming into bright red delicacies. The first cultivars producing decent edible fruits were developed about 300 years ago. Dispersal of the seeds is by birds and mammals, generally rodents, attracted to eat the sweet, juicy fruits.

CHERRY

Deciduous

NATIVE TO *Old World northern hemisphere*
HEIGHT *15 m (49 ft)*
TRUNK DIAMETER *0.5 m (2 ft)*
TRUNK GIRTH *1.6 m (5 ft)*
SPREAD *15 m (49 ft)*

ABOVE *Cherries come in many different kinds, only some of which provide pleasantly edible fruits for human consumption.*

LEFT *A cloud of gorgeous white blossoms decks a mature cherry tree in early spring.*

BLACKTHORN

Prunus spinosa

For much of the year the blackthorn or sloe stands as a small, rather drab tree or hedgerow shrub that, as one of its popular names suggests, involves a tangle of blackish branches and twigs armed with sharp thorns. Yet once a year in the early spring, while the limbs are still bare of leaves, blackthorn metamorphoses into a riot of creamy white, delicate blossoms that provide one of the first banquets of the year for a host of nectar-seeking insects, who in turn serve as pollinators.

The blackthorn is one of the first European native trees to show off its floral finery. Before the leaves unfurl it delivers its welcome splash of glamour to an otherwise grey landscape, generally from late February through the greater part of March, and always before the next wave of white hedgerow colour, usually delivered by the hawthorn in May. Blackthorn grows as a small, sprawling tree, rarely more than 5 metres (16 ft) in height, which is often trimmed back to create a tight and uncompromising stockproof barrier. The tree is very adaptable and will grow in more or less any soil type. Its native range extends from the British Isles right across the length and breadth of Europe, shunning only the more northerly latitudes. It readily throws up suckers and has always been one of the traditional components of a lowland English hedge, usually in company with hawthorn.

The multiple, rather densely arranged stems are clothed with black bark that carries unpleasantly sharp spines or thorns. Individual blossoms are off-white, with five delicate petals surrounding the male and female parts. When the mass of flowers starts to die away, that is the cue for the smallish, somewhat dull and dark green leaves to unfold with their oval shapes and serrated margins. Thus the blackthorn becomes just another thoroughly inconspicuous member of the hedgerow community, a safe refuge for nesting birds, until the autumn approaches when it offers a new attraction.

From August onwards the fruits or sloes become more apparent as they swell and ripen, changing colour from green to a dark purple. In botanical terms the fruit is a drupe made up of a thin, protective outer layer, the 'skin', inside which a juicy, fleshy mass surrounds a 'stone' or endocarp. The endocarp constitutes a hardened inner layer of the fruit, enclosing a single seed. Although the blackthorn is related to the *Prunus* species that produces edible plums, it is not advisable to sample the raw sloes, since they are exceptionally sour. When immersed in gin for a suitable period with sugar, they do, however, impart a unique flavour to create a sloe gin liqueur.

BLACKTHORN

Deciduous

NATIVE TO *Old World northern hemisphere*
HEIGHT *5 m (16 ft)*
TRUNK DIAMETER *0.2 m (1 ft)*
TRUNK GIRTH *0.6 m (2 ft)*
SPREAD *5 m (16 ft)*

ABOVE *Blackthorn flowers early in spring and its blossoms create a fragrant spectacle in hedgerows and thickets.*

LEFT *The profusion of fruits decking the boughs of blackthorn may look tempting to eat, but they are exceptionally sour, and are better suited to making sloe gin.*

DOUGLAS FIR
Pseudotsuga menziesii

A veritable giant of a tree, the massive size of the Douglas fir is exceeded by only one other conifer native to the North American west, the coast redwood. The Latin name of the tree is more accurate, since the species was first documented by the Scottish naturalist, Archibald Menzies, on Vancouver Island in 1791. David Douglas earns the credit for collecting the first seeds from along the Columbia river and sending them back to England more than 30 years later in 1824.

Records indicate that specimen trees of Douglas fir have reached a colossal 120 metres (394 ft) in height. The tallest surviving today is the so-called Doerner fir in Coos County, Oregon, standing at over 99 metres (325 ft). However, in spite of its name, this is not a true fir of the *Abies* genus. So vast are the trunks when fully matured that they can achieve a diameter at the base of 5 metres (16 ft), half the length of a bus. The species also has considerable longevity, commonly living more than 500 years and, in rare instances, double that age. Requiring a moist, mild climate, the tree is native to western North America, its geographical range extending the length of the coast from British Columbia to the Sierra Nevada, and from sea level up to altitudes of 1,800 metres (5,906 ft).

The species tends to prune itself by shedding lower limbs, and although young specimens may have lower branches sweeping the ground, a mature Douglas fir will have become free of branches for at least the first 40 metres (131 ft). A comparatively narrow crown of foliage begins above this height. The trunk of young trees tends to be smooth and grey-green, but as it ages it becomes a dark purplish-brown, clothed in a thick, corky bark with deep, criss-crossed fissures. The foliage takes the form of shortish needles, each about 2.5 centimetres (1 in) in length, arranged in spirals around the pendant young stems but twisted at the base so that they lie in flat rows. If they are crushed, the needles are pleasantly aromatic.

The inflorescence is separately male and female, but both sexes can be found on the same tree, and pollination is by wind. Female cones produced in spring are at first yellow, later becoming light brown, and they hang down from the branches, generally high up in the tree. Each is a slender, oval shape with a pointed tip and soft, three-pronged scales. Production of fertile cones tends not to begin for the first 20 years of the tree's life and the seeds are dispersed on comparatively large single wings.

DOUGLAS FIR

Evergeen

NATIVE TO *West coast of North America*
HEIGHT *95 m (312 ft)*
TRUNK DIAMETER *5 m (16 ft)*
TRUNK GIRTH *16 m (54 ft)*
SPREAD *6 m (20 ft)*

ABOVE *The female cones of the Douglas fir hang from the upper branches, and each bears scales decorated with a spiky, three-pronged tip.*

LEFT *Trunks of gigantic Douglas firs rise from the heavily snowbound floor of Mount Baker-Snoqualmie National Forest, east of Seattle in Washington State, USA.*

HOLM OAK

Quercus ilex

One could be forgiven for assuming that all oaks are deciduous, but worldwide there are at least 27 species of evergreen oak. One of these, the holm oak, although originating from the Mediterranean region, is also now extensively naturalized in other parts of temperate Europe, having been introduced in the 16th century, and in some areas is now classed as an invasive alien.

This is a tree that has become remarkably well adapted to life in latitudes somewhat colder than its balmy Mediterranean native range would indicate. It is most at home in arid climates at low altitudes, where it can form either pure stands or congregate with trees such as cedar in mixed forests. With climate change under way, however, its range is now pushing ever further northwards. It copes equally with pollution from salt spray and urban fumes, but it does not fare well if exposed to severe frost.

Holm oak can reach fairly substantial proportions, growing to a height of 25 metres (82 ft), borne up on a stout trunk and spreading, when mature, into a broad rounded profile with slightly downward sweeping branches that fall low to the ground. Because of its quite imposing evergreen appearance, it is often planted as an ornamental tree in parks and large gardens. There are some particularly massive specimens standing in Kew Gardens, London. The bark is dark and blackish and becomes finely cracked as it ages. The tree earned its botanical name *Quercus ilex* because of the resemblance of the young foliage to the leaves of European holly, *Ilex aquifolium*. The adult leaf is ovate and entire, but in young trees the foliage on the lower branches can bear spiny teeth. The leaves tend to be renewed in spring, and for a few weeks before the upper surface turns a dark glossy green, they are almost silvery-grey in colour.

In late spring the tree produces dense masses of male catkins. From a distance these can give the tree a brief golden sheen, although individually and at close range they appear fairly inconspicuous. Pollination is carried out by wind, and the fruit resulting from fertilization of the female catkin is an acorn, slightly smaller in size than that of the deciduous oaks, which matures and falls from the tree in the autumn.

The wood of holm oak, like that of other members of the genus, is very hard and durable and in Mediterranean countries it has been employed since Roman times to make cartwheels and practical tools. The foliage was also sometimes worked into the leafy crowns worn by Roman emperors to symbolize their divinity.

HOLM OAK

Evergeen

NATIVE TO *The Mediterranean*
HEIGHT *25 m (82 ft)*
TRUNK DIAMETER *1.5 m (5 ft)*
TRUNK GIRTH *4.7 m (15 ft)*
SPREAD *20 m (66 ft)*

ABOVE *The relationship of the holm oak with other members of the oak tree genus is revealed by the familiar shape of the acorn fruits nestling in their small green cups.*

LEFT *The rugged and deeply sculptured trunk of a holm oak is captured in sharp focus on a Spanish hillside.*

ENGLISH or PEDUNCULATE OAK

Quercus robur

This is a mighty tree that breathes a veritable spirit of ruggedness and grit, standing firm against all that the vagaries of nature can throw in its direction. It is not in the character of the oak to shed its leaves hurriedly as the skies begin to darken and the first signs of an autumn tempest whip through its branches. The summer foliage of the oak may still be clinging on resolutely as Christmas approaches.

When stood beside such slender and delicately formed trees as the birch, there is nothing remotely soft about the character of the oak, the monarch of the woodlands. As its limbs finally become bared in winter it is revealed as a truly formidable individual, with massive branches that seem as if they are full of muscle and sinew, twisting and gnarling in all directions. For centuries, the tree has been an integral part of English culture and heritage especially.

Found growing in the wild across most of Europe and as far as the Caucasus, *Quercus robur* reaches a height of 35 metres (115 ft), occasionally more. When fully mature it possesses a magnificently ragged appearance with an open crown of widely spreading, often bent or crooked branches, all clothed in grey, deeply furrowed bark. The oldest specimen trees possess considerable endurance and can live for more than 1,000 years. At such great age they may have developed a considerable girth of more than 12 metres (39 ft) around the base of the trunk. Sometimes in mature trees the branches at the top of the crown die off to create what is known as a 'stag head'. This is usually the outcome of a conservation strategy and not an indication that the tree itself is dying. It points to a tree having suffered water shortage at some time in the past, when it will simply shut off the supply to its own upper extremities.

Most European oak species, with the notable exception of the holm oak, are deciduous, and species can be told apart by the way their leaves are attached. The leaves are always lobed, but the leaf stalks of common or pedunculate oak are very short, almost non-existent compared with those of its cousin, the sessile oak, *Quercus petraea*. This may sound contradictory before it is explained that the terms 'pedunculate' and 'sessile' relate to the stalks bearing the acorn fruits. In the pedunculate oak the acorns are borne on long stalks or peduncles, while in the sessile oak the stalks are lacking. The tree bears catkins from early May to June, and after fertilization the female inflorescence develops into the familiar green acorn sitting in its knobbly cup.

ENGLISH OAK

Deciduous

NATIVE TO *Europe*
HEIGHT *35 m (115 ft)*
TRUNK DIAMETER *3.8 m (12 ft)*
TRUNK GIRTH *12 m (39 ft)*
SPREAD *30 m (98 ft)*

ABOVE *This leaf shape is common to several species of oak, but its very short stalk singles it out as the pedunculate oak, whose name actually refers to the long peduncles of the acorns.*

LEFT *In early winter an English oak, its colours fast changing from green to russet, stands in solitary splendour among arable fields at Lamyatt in the west of England.*

SOUTHERN LIVE OAK

Quercus virginiana

An icon of the Old South, the southern live oak stands silent and serene, breathing history and dripping from every branch with long, feathery tendrils of grey Spanish moss. Native to Virginia, Florida and parts of Texas through to Carolina, Mississippi and the northernmost parts of Mexico, it epitomizes the bygone romance of the American Deep South, of Dixie, Scarlett O'Hara and elegant old colonial society.

Quercus virginiana is known as southern live oak primarily to distinguish it from any of the other evergreen species of oak native to the United States, which may also earn the local name of 'live oak'. It is not a particularly large tree, reaching little more than 15 metres (49 ft), but with a broad spreading habit, the total span of the branches may far exceed the height and reach 45 metres (148 ft). Borne up on a stout trunk clothed with bark that is deeply furrowed lengthwise and darkly coloured brownish-grey, the long branches tend to sweep elegantly downwards before turning up at their extremities, and they bear dense foliage providing a large and welcoming amount of shade.

The tree is fast growing, not wholly evergreen but it retains its greenery for almost 12 months of the year, only shedding its leaves in the spring and growing fresh ones almost immediately. The foliage is coarse and leathery, the leaves dark green above and a paler greyish-green on the slightly downy undersurface. The leaf is reminiscent of that on an English oak, but with a more regular, less wavy outline. Much as with other oaks, the male flowers are greenish catkins that mature up to 10 centimetres (4 in) long, pollinated by wind during April, and the fruit arising from the female inflorescence during the autumn is a small, tapering acorn.

One of the features most strongly associated with the southern live oak is the long, tendrilly epiphytes that hang in festoons from the branches of many of the trees. Although these growths are popularly referred to as Spanish moss they are, in fact, flowering plants similar to 'air plants'.

The oldest living specimen tree stands in Middleton, South Carolina, claimed to be a veteran of over 1,500 years. This, however, is an unsubstantiated estimate and when in 2008 part of the crown collapsed, its growth rings were counted suggesting that it probably first took root in about the middle of the 15th century. One of the most magnificent plantations of southern live oak surviving from colonial times is an imposing double row of 28 of the trees at Vacherie in Louisiana.

SOUTHERN LIVE OAK

Deciduous

NATIVE TO *Southern North America*
HEIGHT *15 m (49 ft)*
TRUNK DIAMETER *2 m (7 ft)*
TRUNK GIRTH *6.25 m (21 ft)*
SPREAD *Up to 45 m (148 ft)*

ABOVE *The leaves of the southern live oak possess a similar shape to those of the English oak, but are leathery and arranged fan-wise, with a more regular outline.*

LEFT *Live oak trunks and boughs, dripping with grey Spanish moss, exude the spirit of the American Deep South.*

RED MANGROVE

Rhizophora mangle

Red mangrove is a coastal species growing very close to the water's edge, if not with its feet in water. The term 'rhizophore' means literally a root stem and gives a clue to the remarkable adaptation of the tree to its unique habitat. From the main trunk it develops numerous thin, aerial prop roots that angle down into the surrounding mud to give it anchoring support, and this unusual feature tends to the separate the species from other types of mangrove.

The tree is native to the tropical and subtropical regions of both hemispheres, and it sometimes becomes an invasive pest when it spreads in dense thickets across river estuaries and mudflats that can prove inhospitable to many other plants. The tree is nonetheless of considerable value ecologically, in that it reduces erosion by acting as a buffer against tropical storms and the constant wearing action of tides. For this reason, it is often planted to improve coastal stability. The trees also effectively recycle nutrients through their leaf fall, and provide an invaluable refuge for inshore fish, invertebrates and nesting waders.

Individuals can sometimes attain a moderately substantial height of up 25 metres (82 ft), although generally they remain shorter. They are physiologically adapted to spend much of their lives with roots submerged in salt water, the sandy mud or clay in which they grow only exposed at low tide, if at all. The aerial roots thus play an additional role in assisting gas exchange with the atmosphere when large parts of the tree are submerged.

Red mangrove rises up on a comparatively slender trunk, clothed with thin, greyish bark that becomes thicker and more furrowed with age. It is an evergreen species that sheds its foliage periodically, and the leaves are of a simple ovate shape, up to 12 centimetres (5 in) long, glossy dark green above and more yellowish below, with an absence of obvious veining. Out of necessity, the foliage is thick and leathery so as to resist the drying effects of salt.

In spring the tree produces unremarkable pale yellow flowers and is wind pollinated. Its method of propagation is, however, rather more remarkable because it has 'fruits' that resemble seed pods, but which are actually individual baby trees, known botanically as propagules. These mature on the tree and when ripe are then capable of rooting directly as fresh plants. In other words, there is no dormant seed stage: the propagule evolves from flower to new plant continuously while attached to the parent. The propagules will also float on water, and can exist in this fashion for more than a year before finding a suitable place to put out their first roots.

RED MANGROVE

Evergreen

NATIVE TO *Tropical and subtropical regions*
HEIGHT *25 m (82 ft)*
TRUNK DIAMETER *0.4 m (1 ft)*
TRUNK GIRTH *1.25 m (4 ft)*
SPREAD *20 m (66 ft)*

ABOVE *The typical arrangement of a slender trunk topped by a bushy canopy and a profusion of prop roots that anchor the tree to the tidal mudflat.*

LEFT *A red mangrove on the Queensland coast of Australia develops large numbers of thin, aerial prop roots that help support its main trunk in unstable shifting sands.*

GIANT RHODODENDRON
Rhododendron grande

There are many exquisite flowering trees to be searched out growing in the world's more remote fastnesses, but few can compare with the giant rhododendron when it is decked out in full bloom. For the intrepid explorer taking an arduous path up through the densely clothed foothills of the Himalaya in the tiny states of Sikkim and Bhutan, this is a prize well worth the journey.

ts native range restricted to the eastern end of the Himalaya, this tree in the wild does not necessarily compare with the neat, cultivated shrubs to be found in parks and gardens. The aptly named giant rhododendron can grow on the lower mountain slopes to a height of 10 metres (33 ft) and it becomes the dominant species in hilly forests, thriving at altitudes of up to 3,000 metres (9,843 ft). Even in cultivation some specimen trees of more than 40 years of age have been known to reach 8 metres (26 ft) tall, attaining a similar width. Being a woodland plant it requires a steady supply of moisture in the soil, but it is fairly hardy against mild frosts.

Tending to develop with multiple stems, the tree then branches prolifically into a broad, shrubby profile. The foliage takes the form of large, distinctive leaves that are leathery, glossy green on the upper surface, silvery-grey below, narrowly ovate in profile and up to 45 centimetres (18 in) in length with very marked midribs and veins. In spring the new young foliage can be pretty, with pinkish bracts and a silky covering. The size of the leaves means that the foliage can readily become damaged by strong winds and scorched by prologed exposure to direct sunlight. Thus giant rhododendron fares best in sheltered sites with dappled shade provided by other taller trees.

The flowers are, of course, the tree's crowning glory. In the northern hemisphere they emerge from February to April depending on the temperature, in loose trusses or corymbs of up to 25 densely packed individual blooms. Each flower is bell shaped, up to 8 centimetres (3 in) long with eight lobes and 16 stamens. At the bud stage the flower is a pale rose colour, but once opened it becomes creamy white with a dark purple patch forming a nectary at the base of the corolla tube. The tree does not generally blossom until it is about 12 years old, but then erupts with such large masses of blooms that the plant can be severely weakened by the energy put into their production. The fruit is an elongated capsule.

GIANT RHODODENDRON

Evergreen

NATIVE TO *Himalayan foothills*
HEIGHT *10 m (33 ft)*
TRUNK DIAMETER *0.3 m (1 ft)*
TRUNK GIRTH *0.95 m (3 ft)*
SPREAD *15 m (49 ft)*

ABOVE *Each snowy-white blossom bears a darker, purplish patch that marks out the position of a nectary at the base of the corolla tube.*

LEFT *Giant rhododendrons create a delightful spectacle, with big, showy white blooms that typically grace the lower slopes in the Himalayas.*

WEEPING WILLOW

Salix babylonica

This graceful tree with its familiar romantic beauty will also be known to many people for its inclusion in the Biblical Old Testament. In the words of Psalm 137: 'By the rivers of Babylon, there we sat down, yea, wept, when we remembered Zion. We hanged our harps upon the willows in the midst thereof.' In spite of its botanical name, however, the weeping willow was probably not originally native to the ancient Near East, but rather to the drier central Asian parts of western and northern China.

The original wild form of the tree, Beijing willow or *Salix matsudana*, tends not to be very succesfully grown outside China, nor is it especially 'weeping'. At some time in antiquity, the precise date long since lost but probably several thousand years ago, the cultivar that we now call weeping willow was developed. This was eventually called *Salix babylonica* in 1736 by the botanist Carl Linnaeus, who named it in error, wrongly assuming the tree of Biblical fame to be of Mesopotamian origin. By the time of Nebuchadnezzar it had been spread westwards from China along the ancient trade routes, and been planted extensively on the banks of the Tigris and Euphrates rivers. Most of the pendulous weeping varieties of *Salix babylonica* familiar in Europe and North America today are actually hybrids that have been developed with better tolerance of comparatively damp climatic conditions and frosts in temperate latitudes, although they are still prone to cankers and fungal infection. The first weeping willows were introduced to England from Syria in 1730, and one of the most popular forms today is *Salix babylonica* var. *tortuosa*, commonly dubbed 'wiggly willow' because of its contorted stems and slightly twisted leaves.

The mature tree can reach 20 metres (66 ft) tall, with an elegantly rounded crown, although generally it achieves little more than half this height. It is capable of growing rapidly, but the wood is comparatively weak; as a result, it often has a short lifespan. Nonetheless, some specimen trees are known to have been growing for a hundred years or more, developing massive girth at the base of the trunk. The branches tend to project fairly horizontally outward, but the masses of thinner yellow-brown young stems characteristically hang down to the ground in pendulous curtains to create the distinctive and graceful form. Bearing spirally arranged, narrow, lance-like leaves up to 15 centimetres (6 in) long with pointed tips and finely serrated margins that fall late in the autumn, the flowers are insignificant yellow catkins.

WEEPING WILLOW

Deciduous

NATIVE TO *Northern China*
HEIGHT *20 m (66 ft)*
TRUNK DIAMETER *0.6 m (2 ft)*
TRUNK GIRTH *1.8 m (6 ft)*
SPREAD *20 m (66 ft)*

ABOVE *In spring, before the leaves unfold, all willows bear furry catkins.*

LEFT *A graceful weeping willow, its leaf colour fading at the close of summer, stands serenely with its branches forming a curtain over an ornamental lake.*

ELDER

Sambucus nigra

Also called the black elder to distinguish it from other species of *Sambucus*, this is a small tree or shrub that has been revered for centuries on account of its medicinal properties. It has also been regularly attributed with magical powers, and is still subject to local superstitions on account of the medieval and purely fictional story that Judas Escariot hung himself from an elder tree. Alas, the tree is not native to Biblical Palestine and would certainly be unable to support the weight of a man.

Short lived and sometimes untidy in its appearance, the elder is a deciduous tree or shrub native to temperate and subtropical regions and found throughout much of Europe, western Asia and north Africa, as well as parts of the southern hemisphere including South America and Australia. It is an opportunist that will quickly colonize any disturbed soil or waste ground as well as woodlands generally, roadsides and railway embankments.

The tree can grow to a height of about 8 metres (26 ft), with spreading, somewhat arching branches, and prefers sunny locations. When its light is blocked out by other more dominant woodland trees, elder can often remain small and straggly with long, thin stems. When young, the trunk and boughs are clothed in smooth, pale grey bark that becomes pregressively darker and more seamed as it ages. In spite of the fact that the branches break very readily, the heartwood of the trunk can actually be very hard. The foliage, which tends to give off an unpleasant pungent aroma reminiscent of mice, takes the form of compound leaves, each consisting of five to seven individual leaflets that are ovate with serrated edges and arranged in pairs with a single terminal leaflet.

In May the tree blossoms with a riot of small, creamy-white flowers packed together in broad, pretty clusters or panicles, and there is an old country saying that summer has not properly arrived until the elder is in bloom. The flowers are pollinated by insects. In the autumn the fruits ripen as familiar clusters of purple or black berries, much sought after by hungry birds and makers of homemade wine.

The name *Sambucus* has a curious origin, possibly tracing back to a Greek word, 'sambuca'. This may have described an ancient wind instrument invented by the Romans from the hollowed-out stems of the tree, and introduced to Europe as the 'sackbut'. In modern Italy a rustic pipe called a *sampogna* is still to be found made from elder stems. There is a question mark over the theory of Greek beginnings, however, because the name 'sambuca' also refers to a stringed instrument.

ELDER

Deciduous

NATIVE TO *Europe, western Asia, north Africa*
HEIGHT *8 m (26 ft)*
TRUNK DIAMETER *0.2 m (1 ft)*
TRUNK GIRTH *0.6 m (2 ft)*
SPREAD *8 m (26 ft)*

ABOVE *Elderberries hang in a dense, shiny cluster awaiting attention from birds stocking up on fare before the onset of winter.*

LEFT *An elder tree in full bloom lends its brilliant splash of creamy white to the greenery of a waterside hedge bank.*

SANDALWOOD

Santalum album

For more than 2,000 years, the fragrant oil extracted from the wood of this somewhat untidy tropical tree, native to the southern parts of India, Indonesia and northern Australia, has been sought after and occasionally fought over. It is valued not only as a beguiling and luxurious commodity in the cosmetic trade, but also for its use in religious practices, especially those of Hinduism.

Often growing on poor sandy or rocky soils up to altitudes of 1,200 metres (3,937 ft) among scrub vegetation, the sandalwood tree is not a free-living plant but a partial parasite that attaches during the growing stages of its life to the roots of other host species, on which it depends for supplies of water and mineral salts. However, the sandalwood behaves otherwise as a normal green plant, reliant on sunlight for the production of its food, so the host plants have to be of a type that will not deprive it of essential daylight. To this end the parasitic roots of the sandalwood can extend a good 10 metres (33 ft) from the base of the tree, thus minimizing the chance of overcrowding by the host. There are around 300 species of plant that can be parasitized by sandalwood, and although host species have not been exhaustively identified, saplings are often grown commercially in combination with *Capsicum* species (chilli pepper).

In the Indian subcontinent sandalwood can attain a height of 20 metres (66 ft), but the trees that are found growing in Australia rarely exceed 4 metres (13 ft), and the species may not actually be indigenous there. Some theories suggest that it was carried to Australia in antiquity by boat people. An evergreen, its slender, drooping branches spread from a stout trunk clothed in dark reddish bark that is smooth in young trees but later roughened and seamed. The foliage arises in opposite pairs of leaves, ovate, smooth and glossy green above, slightly more blue-green below. The flowers bloom in small, inconspicuous clusters or panicles, from March to April in India and at different times in the other areas. The fruit that follows fertilization is a rounded drupe, at first green, then becoming purple or black when ripe, and the seeds are dispersed by birds feeding on the fleshy outer parts.

The sandalwood tree can live for 100 years or more, but not surprisingly has suffered from centuries of over-exploitation on account of its scented wood and the oils it produces. It has also been severely depleted in its native range by scrub clearance for agriculture and by fire, and is now a protected species worldwide. The Indian government has placed a ban on export in an attempt to curb widespread illegal felling.

SANDALWOOD

Evergreen

NATIVE TO *Europe, western Asia, north Africa*
HEIGHT *20 m (66 ft)*
TRUNK DIAMETER *0.75 m (2 ft)*
TRUNK GIRTH *2.4 m (8 ft)*
SPREAD *18 m (59 ft)*

ABOVE *The leaves of the sandalwood are evergreen, smoothly regular, with a glossy surface.*

LEFT *A mature sandalwood tree reaches skywards, borne up on a stout, seamed trunk at Jawa on the island of Timor, Indonesia.*

AFRICAN VIOLET TREE

Securidaca longepedunculata

Not to be confused with the small herbaceous flowering plant of the same common name, this is a pretty, comparatively small tree whose native range is extensive and includes much of tropical Africa. Its popular use as a medicinal plant, however, has resulted in considerable reduction of trees and it is now a threatened species, especially in Mali where it has fallen victim to unregulated harvesting. The tree has been made a protected species in many areas of South Africa and Mozambique.

Growing to little more than 10 metres (33 ft) in height, the African violet tree could equally be described as a large shrub that is most commonly found in open savannah woodland, mainly in the south and west of the continent. It can survive equally well in situations ranging from hot, dry, subtropical bush to dense equatorial rainforests and narrow gallery forests along the banks of rivers up to altitudes of 800 metres (2,625 ft). It prefers its roots to be in sandy soils, and has developed good resistance to bush fires. It will also cope with limited periods of drought. So popular is the tree for its medicinal properties that in parts of Nigeria it is known as *uwar magunguna*, meaning 'mother of medicines'. The roots provide the greatest concentration of medicinal properties, and this has been the main cause of its disturbing reduction in numbers.

The trunk is clothed with smooth, pale grey bark and branches profusely into a rather straggly, open crown of limb. The evergreen leaves are borne on short, spiny-tipped side branches and either alternate on the stem or sprout in clusters from the tips. They can vary considerably in size and shape, from thinly elliptical to quite broad with rounded ends. The leaf surfaces are finely downy when young but become bare or glabrous as the leaf ages.

The tree blossoms at the beginning of the rainy season with small but very pretty pinkish-violet flowers, which are reminiscent of sweet peas in appearance and are borne in clusters in the axils of the youngest leaves. The way the flowers are borne gives rise to the *longepedunculata* part of the name, because the individuals are carried on elongated stalks or peduncles. Each flower is made up of five sepals, of which the two lateral members are large and petal like. These protect three true petals, the middle member of which is hooked like a keel. The fruit is a nut whose outer coat becomes extended into a curved wing and thus looks not unlike the samara of a sycamore.

AFRICAN VIOLET TREE

Deciduous (briefly)

NATIVE TO *Europe, western Asia, north Africa*
HEIGHT *10 m (33 ft)*
TRUNK DIAMETER *0.4 m (1 ft)*
TRUNK GIRTH *1.25 m (4 ft)*
SPREAD *12 m (39 ft)*

ABOVE *A young African violet tree, inconspicuous without its flowers, may easily be overlooked.*

LEFT *The pretty pink blossoms offer a brief but charming spectacle at the start of the rainy season.*

COAST REDWOOD

Sequoia sempervirens

The tallest living organism in the world, this tree in its full maturity is truly an awesome spectacle. Restricted to the west coast of North America in the states of California and Oregon, it is related to another giant of the forest, the wellingtonia. In 2006, a coast redwood given the name Hyperion in the Redwood National Park in California was measured at 115 metres (377 ft). Laid on the ground, it would reach 10 metres (33 ft) beyond the length of an official international soccer pitch.

The species was first discovered in 1769, but its botanical description had to wait another 50 years before being compiled. Since that time, some 96 per cent of redwoods in their native range have been destroyed through logging, although the tree is now a protected species and those grown for timber production are all cultivated in plantations. *Sequoia* honours a Cherokee chief of that name in the early 19th century, who devised a means of writing his native language. A type of cypress, coast redwood is the only surviving species within the genus. Capable of great longevity, the tree can live for more than 2,000 years and although Hyperion is the tallest living specimen known, there are unsubstantiated records of even taller trees, including one that was felled in 1886 measuring a little over 129 metres (423 ft).

The tree demands a moist, equable climate, hence its natural limitation to a narrow coastal strip on slopes facing the sea, which are often shrouded in fog. The tallest specimens are generally located in deep valleys, where there is a year-long preponderance of damp air and flowing water. For a considerable part of its height the massive trunk is bare of branches, since it prunes itself and it is generally buttressed at the base. Supported on very wide-spreading, shallow roots, its dimensions can be truly colossal, up to almost 8 metres (26 ft) in diameter. The bark, with age, becomes immensely thick and fibrous, up to 30 centimetres (12 in) deep and heavily sculptured. Where it breaks away, the underlying bark is rich reddish-brown, giving the tree its name 'redwood'. Above 25 metres (82 ft) or more, a mature coast redwood expands into a loose, fairly narrow crown with horizontal or slightly drooping branches. The foliage varies from being long and flat on young trees, to small and scaly on the upper parts of mature trees where the branches are in full sun.

Male and female cones are produced separately on the same tree and pollination is by wind, but coast redwood also reproduces itself vegetatively by sprouting from the roots and stumps and fallen timber. For this reason trees often appear to grow in straight lines, whereas they have, in fact, taken root all along the length of an old, felled trunk.

COAST REDWOOD

Evergreen

NATIVE TO *West coast of North America*
HEIGHT *115 m (377 ft)*
TRUNK DIAMETER *8 m (26 ft)*
TRUNK GIRTH *25 m (82 ft)*
SPREAD *13 m (43 ft)*

ABOVE *Long, flat needles characterize the foliage of young coast redwood trees before becoming small and scaly.*

LEFT *Misty sunlight penetrating the Redwood National Park in California gives these colossal coast redwoods an almost surreal appearance.*

Walking among the coast redwoods in Redwood National Park gives you the true sense of scale of these enormous wonders of nature.

WELLINGTONIA

Sequoiadendron giganteum

This is a tree of awe-inspiring beauty, and if the colossal bulk that it can attain is to be any measure, it is the largest living thing on Earth. For many people, to stand quietly, alone, in a grove of wellingtonia becomes a humbling experience. Surrounded by gigantic pure columns that soar into the heavens, one has entered a place akin to a living cathedral.

The only surviving member of the genus *Sequoiadendron*, the wellingtonia is an evergreen conifer within the group known as 'redwoods'. Its native range is restricted to scattered groves on the seaward-facing slopes of the Sierra Nevada in California, most notably in the Yosemite National Park, and the statistics of the tree speak for themselves. Exceptionally large specimen trees have been known to reach over 90 metres (295 ft) in height and a vast 17 metres (56 ft) in diameter. The fibrous and deeply fissured red bark may in itself be almost 1 metre (3 ft) thick at the base of the trunk, and this provides it with a degree of effective fire protection. Where fire damage has occurred the trunk will also readily sprout new branches in its lower half although, unlike the coast redwood, *Sequoia sempervirens*, a cut stump will not produce new growth.

In profile, a young tree keeps fairly regular and conical in shape, but as it ages the appearance becomes more open and ragged, the comparatively short horizontal limbs, massive as they are, seemingly disproportionate to the immense size of the trunk. This may become wholly bare at heights beneath 50 metres (164 ft) after the branches die off and fall as a result of shading, and the base of the trunk may be hugely buttressed, resembling a gnarled giant's foot. Sometimes the apex of the crown in old trees shears off in storms and is replaced by new limbs that point upwards, thus creating a more flattened top. The oldest known wellingtonia is about 3,500 years old – at least 1,000 years older than the Greek Parthenon.

The foliage is blue-green and scaly, either closely pressed against the stems or more spreading depending on position. Inflorescence is produced in the spring in the form of separate male and female cones, mostly confined to the upper third of the tree, and pollination is by wind. Even the cone statistics are impressive. A single cone up to 7 centimetres (3 in) long can produce over 200 seeds, and a big wellingtonia may at any one time be carrying 11,000 cones, dispersing more than a quarter of a million seeds in a season.

WELLINGTONIA

Evergreen

NATIVE TO *West coast of North America*
HEIGHT *90 m (295 ft)*
TRUNK DIAMETER *17 m (56 ft)*
TRUNK GIRTH *53 m (174 ft)*
SPREAD *30 m (98 ft)*

ABOVE *Once ripe, this as yet undeveloped female cone, hanging from the topmost branches of a wellingtonia, can produce over 200 seeds.*

LEFT *The awesome dimensions of a wellingtonia standing in Grant Grove in the Sequoia National Park, California, make neighbouring fully grown conifers look puny by comparison.*

ROWAN

Sorbus aucuparia

Also known rather confusingly as mountain ash, this species is wholly unrelated to the true ash trees, which belong to the *Fraxinus* genus. It earns the title merely because its leaves resemble those of the ash and from an ability to thrive at high altitudes. In fact, it is a member of the rose family. Its more obscure name, rowan, is thought to be a corruption of an Old Norse word for the tree, *raun*, which in turn may derive from *raudnian* meaning 'becoming red' and referring to the bright scarlet berries.

The rowan is native to more or less all the cooler temperate regions of the northern hemisphere, where it survives at altitudes of up to 1,000 metres (3,281 ft), higher than any other broad-leaved trees will tolerate; further south, in the French Alps, it can be found at almost 2,000 metres (6,562 ft). It is not too fussy about soil conditions, and on windswept exposed hillsides the tree may end up as little more than a stunted and gnarled bush, frequently taking root in crevices between rocks, and occasionally surviving for a year or so as an epiphyte in the cleft of an old conifer. But at lower levels and in more sheltered sites, it will grow to as much as 20 metres (66 ft) or more in height.

For centuries associated with witchcraft and the supernatural, *Sorbus aucuparia* has also been called the 'wicken tree' or 'rune tree'. In spite of its hardiness the tree has a comparatively short lifespan, but it is an opportunist that grows fast, developing a slender, fairly open profile with upwardly angled branches clothed in smooth, grey-brown bark. Rowan is deciduous and in April bears compound leaves arranged as narrow, serrated leaflets in opposite pairs of up to 14, with one terminal leaflet. The foliage turns a vivid orange-red before it is abandoned in autumn.

Flowers appear from May to early June after the leaves have unfurled, in dense creamy-white clusters or corymbs, each of which can include up to 250 small individual blooms about 1 centimetre (0.4 in) across and containing both male and female parts. They are strongly scented and pollination is by a wide variety of insects. The rowan is best known for its pretty clusters of bright red 'berries'. In botanical terms these fruits are pomes, each containing up to eight seeds that develop in autumn and provide a feast for birds stocking up before the onset of winter. The seeds are thus effectively dispersed in their droppings.

ROWAN

Deciduous

NATIVE TO *Temperate regions of the northern hemisphere*
HEIGHT *20 m (66 ft)*
TRUNK DIAMETER *0.5 m (2 ft)*
TRUNK GIRTH *1.6 m (5 ft)*
SPREAD *14 m (46 ft)*

ABOVE *Berries arise in red clusters and provide a much-needed feast for overwintering birds.*

LEFT *A rowan, blasted and bent over many seasons by the uncompromising elements, stands defiantly on an exposed hillside.*

AFRICAN TULIP TREE

Spathodea campanulata

With its native range confined to the rainforests of equatorial Africa, this is a solitary tree on its own, the sole member of its genus. It is also an invasive opportunist that will quickly take root in land left unattended, and is therefore sometimes regarded as an unwelcome pest. It is, however, also a great favourite throughout the tropics as a flowering ornamental and has now spread as a naturalized escapee in many parts of the Pacific region, including the hotter areas of northern Australia.

A lso sometimes called the 'flame of the forest', *Spathodea campanulata* is not to be confused with *Butea monosperma*, whose native range lies in India and is from a different group of plants. *Spathodea* is found chiefly in rainforests and is a fast-growing, moderately tall deciduous tree that reaches 25 metres (82 ft) in height and occasionally 35 metres (115 ft). It generally favours elevations below 900 metres (2,953 ft) on moist sites in seltered valleys, but can sometimes be found ascending to 1,200 metres (3,937 ft) on drier slopes. Where it finds suitable accommodation, it can quickly form dense thickets that shade out most other vegetation.

It grows up on a massive, rather tapering, light grey-brown trunk with short, spreading limbs that are also thickly constructed. The bark may be either smooth or finely furry, coupled with a somewhat warty appearance created by prominent raised breathing pores or lenticels, but it becomes darker, scaly and full of fissures as the tree ages. The compound pinnate leaves are made up of as many as 19 oval leaflets, pointed at the tips, and all oppositely arranged with the addition of a terminal leaflet. The leaves are bronze in colour when they open, but soon mature to a deep, glossy green with prominent yellow midribs and networks of veins.

It is, however, the ornate flowers that capture the most attention. Large and flame red with orange interiors, they contain both male and female parts and possess an appearance reminiscent of tulips, from whence one of the popular names originates. The flowers unfold from buds shaped like curved, velvety, bronze-green bananas, pointing upwards, that are clustered at the end of the branches and hold water that readily squirts out when they are squeezed or punctured. When about to open, the buds of the outer tier bend away from the bunch and erupt into large orange and red bells with frilly edges, streaked with gold inside. Generally pollinated by birds in search of nectar, the resultant fruit takes the form of a long, greenish-brown fingerlike capsule that points upwards and outwards clear of the leaves, releasing its seeds about five months after flowering.

AFRICAN TULIP TREE

Evergreen

NATIVE TO *Tropical Africa*
HEIGHT *25 m (82 ft)*
TRUNK DIAMETER *0.5 m (2 ft)*
TRUNK GIRTH *1.6 m (5 ft)*
SPREAD *22 m (72 ft)*

ABOVE *The ornate, flame-red flowers arise in dense clusters at the tips of the branches.*

LEFT *A mature African tulip tree, its blooms in their full fiery splendour, rises spectacularly above the surrounding verdure at Trafalgar in the Dominican Republic.*

WEST INDIAN MAHOGANY

Swietenia mahagoni

This species is one of three closely related subtropical trees found in a New World native range that extends from southern Florida to Bolivia. It was, however, the first of the true mahogany trees to be exported to Europe for its much-prized timber, and this attribute has almost been its nemesis, bringing it close to extinction as a result of over-felling. It is protected in many of its indigenous areas, although the trees are now being grown commercially as a timber crop in a number of Asian countries.

The *Swietenia* species, each native to a geographically distinct area but hybridizing readily when they are grown in close proximity to one another, are all imposing trees, regularly growing to 35 metres (115 ft) and occasionally as much as 45 metres (148 ft) in height. West Indian mahogany is now restricted to the upper Florida Keys and the Everglades National Park, having been eliminated from other more northerly parts of the state through decades of unregulated logging. Aside from the worth of its timber, it is valued as an ornamental in parks and along roadsides, and it is tolerant of both strong winds and salt spray from the ocean.

The trees display a comparatively short length of swollen or buttressed trunk before spreading into a massively rounded profile, created from a profusion of heavy boughs. Not truly evergreen, the leaves fall at the end of the winter season and are absent for only a short period before new foliage appears, so the mahoganies almost always provide extensive shade. The foliage leaves are a purple colour as they unfurl from the buds, but soon become light green. These leaves are unique among deciduous North American trees in that they are pinnate, with three or fours pairs of asymmetrical leaflets but without the usual terminal leaflet. The flowers, borne on new growth at the same time as the emerging leaves, are fragrant, although small and not particularly striking. Even so, the mahogany blossom has been adopted as the national flower of the Dominican Republic. The fruits are woody, pear-shaped capsules, each with five lobes, and they persist on the tree for about a year until the following spring. Seeds are small, winged and dispersed on the winds.

It is, however, the wood of the mahogany that earns the tree its fame. Most of that used commercially today is extracted from a related species, the Honduran mahogany, *Swietenia macrophylla*, which grows somewhat larger and is found across a wider range of South American forests. Sought after for hundreds of years by the best European cabinet makers, mahogany wood is fine grained, very durable and attractively reddish in colour.

WEST INDIAN MAHOGANY

Deciduous

NATIVE TO *Subtropical New World*
HEIGHT *45 m (148 ft)*
TRUNK DIAMETER *2 m (7 ft)*
TRUNK GIRTH *6.25 m (21 ft)*
SPREAD *30 m (98 ft)*

ABOVE *The woody, pear-shaped fruits are constructed in lobes that will split open when ripe to release the wind-blown seeds.*

LEFT *Like its African counterpart, the West Indian mahogany has been over-exploited for timber. Here, however, young trees are grown as a sustainable crop in a Hawaiian plantation.*

TAMARIND

Tamarindus indica

The tamarind is a rather inconspicuous bushy tree of the tropics, bearing unremarkable flowers. Its beauty lies not in dramatic blossoms or impressive girth, but in a much sought-after commodity that it bears on its boughs. For this reason, although in antiquity its native range was probably limited to east Africa, it is now cultivated more or less anywhere in the world that climate permits on account of the flavour contained in its sausage-shaped fruits.

The species name *indica* is misleading and results from an incorrect assumption that the tamarind tree was native to India, where it became naturalized as a result of import in the distant past. It is thought originally to have been indigenous to parts of east Africa, especially the Sudan, where it can still be found growing wild. However, it has a culinary value that was well known even to the ancient Egyptians, and this quickly resulted in dispersal for cultivation throughout the tropics and subtropics from South America to southeast Asia and northern Australia. Arab traders were probably the first to carry it in their saddlebags to Persia and thence India. Much later, during the 16th century, the Spanish colonists introduced it to Mexico, and at about the same time the Portuguese carried its seeds into parts of South America.

Strictly a tree of tropical climes, the tamarind is unable to cope with frost. It is a long-lived and slow-growing evergreen that can eventually reach a height of 25 metres (82 ft), borne up on a massive trunk clothed with rough, dark grey bark. The trunk may attain a girth of as much as 7 metres (23 ft) at its base, and the tree develops a rounded profile, often as wide as it is tall. The foliage carried on stout, slightly drooping branches is bright green and delicate, with a rather feathery appearance created by pinnate leaves consisting of up to 20 pairs of narrowly ovate leaflets, shed occasionally.

Tamarind flowers are not especially noteworthy; each is small and yellowish with orange splashes, and the individual blossoms are borne in clusters or racemes. The all-important fruits that result from fertilization are bean-like pods up to 15 centimetres (6 in) long that hang in profusion from the new stem growth. The maturing pods have a distinctive knobbly appearance, cinnamon brown and looking like sausages stuffed with table-tennis balls. As they ripen, the pods become filled with a juicy, acidic pulp and the outer skin turns into a brittle shell. It is this pulp, when dried to a sticky consistency, that constitutes the tamarind paste so highly valued as a culinary ingredient.

TAMARIND

Evergreen

NATIVE TO *Subtropical Africa*
HEIGHT *25 m (82 ft)*
TRUNK DIAMETER *2.25 m (7 ft)*
TRUNK GIRTH *7 m (23 ft)*
SPREAD *25 m (82 ft)*

ABOVE *The curious fruit pod of the tamarind looks, for all the world, like an oversized, curly version of the broad bean.*

LEFT *The delicate, feathery foliage of a tamarind tree provides a contrasting foreground against the rugged mountain backdrop in Laos, southeast Asia.*

BALD CYPRESS
Taxodium distichum

One should not be deceived by the inauspicious name of the bald cypress. Also known as the swamp cypress, it is one of a limited number of deciduous conifers that become bare of foliage in winter. This, however, is a grand, truly impressive conifer that can ascend 40 metres (131 ft) above its swampland environment. With its gracious profile reflected in dark, tranquil waters, it is an indelible feature of the Everglades and the great swamps that once covered much of the southeastern United States.

The tree regularly grows to a height of 40 metres (131 ft), but occasionally specimen trees exceed this height. The tallest known today stands at a magnificent 44 metres (144 ft) near Williamsburg, Virginia. It has reached a colossal diameter at the base of more than 5 metres (16 ft). Bald cypress also achieves remarkable longevity. Some standing along the edge of the Black river in North Carolina were estimated by dendrologists in the late 1980s to date back as early as 364 CE, making them close to 1,700 years old. In the distant past, the species extended across a much greater global range, and there is fossil evidence that such giant trees once clothed part of southern England.

Bald cypress possesses an unusual feature that is sometimes seen in other swamp trees, but which may be absent when it grows on dried land. Massive adventitious roots known as 'cypress knees' arise from the trunk above water level and angle down into the soil to provide greater support to the enormous weight of timber that the rooting system is required to stabilize. From these buttresses the trunk soars aloft, clothed in reddish-brown, fibrous and deeply fissured bark. The boughs are decked with fine, feathery needles borne on deciduous shoots. They arise in a spiral arrangement but are twisted at the needle base so that they lie in flat rows. The shoots with the needles fall in autumn, but for a few weeks before they are shed they turn from their summer green and provide a rich blaze of fiery red colour.

Both male catkins and female cones are borne on the same tree and pollination is by wind. Catkins are produced on the ends of the shoots and reach 10 centimetres (4 in) long, turning yellowish as they mature. The female cones are somewhat egg shaped, at first green with their scales tightly packed, but becoming purple and woody as they ripen. The scales then spread open in autumn to release their seeds with appendages that act as tiny sails, enabling the seeds to float on the water currents until they find a suitable spot to germinate. The timber of the bald cypress, not surprisingly, is water resistant and is used for a variety of constructions where the wood is likely to be regularly wetted.

BALD CYPRESS

Evergreen

NATIVE TO *Southeastern North America*
HEIGHT *40 m (131 ft)*
TRUNK DIAMETER *5.2 m (17 ft)*
TRUNK GIRTH *16 m (52 ft)*
SPREAD *25 m (82 ft)*

ABOVE *The incredible bald cypress, supported by aerial prop roots, grows seemingly from the bottom of this lake in the Everglades, Florida.*

LEFT *The majestic, deeply fissured trunk soars upwards from its swampy bed.*

Some of the oldest bald cypress trees ever found grow at Bluff Lake, Mississippi. These mysterious trees can reach ages of 1,500 and even 2,000 years. Only a select few tree species worldwide have been proven to live for more than 1,500 years.

EUROPEAN YEW

Taxus baccata

Dark and squat, sunlight rarely penetrating its boughs, the yew is a brooding presence softened only by an occasional dusting of jolly red berries. Not surprisingly, the tree has held an extraordinary place in our hearts and minds almost as far back as recorded human history goes. Growing predominantly on chalk and limestone throughout much of Europe, the trees often attain great longevity. Slow growing and immensely durable, they possess the unique ability to develop fresh trunks from within the decaying mass of the old.

A smallish evergreen conifer with a fairly compact, rounded appearance clothed in dark green, glossy, lance-shaped leaves, the individual trees are dioecious, hence either male or female. The golden male cones shed pollen in early spring; as the fertilized female cones develop, they become enclosed in a fleshy coat, the aril. At maturity, these turn alluringly bright red and juicy, attracting birds to feed. This makes for an efficient dispersal mechanism, because the seeds are passed out in the bird's droppings.

The wood of the yew is hard and durable, but the tree also possesses an extraordinary ability to regenerate. Although resistant to infection, the heartwood eventually succumbs to rot and the tree collapses under its own weight. But from around the decay of the old trunk arise saplings of the new, and this ability contributes to the tree's longevity. A yew in the churchyard of Fortingall in Perthshire, Scotland, is reliably estimated to be more than 2,000 years old, making it the oldest known tree in Europe. Although, sadly, its original trunk collapsed in 1770, now replaced by several separate trunks, its girth was recorded in 1769 at a colossal 16 metres (52 ft). A stripling by comparison, a mere 1,000 years of age and a slender 7 metres (23 ft) around, is the 'Teixu l'Iglesia' at Bermiego in Spain.

The ancient Celts loved their yews. In one of the earliest known European legal documents, the Brehon Laws, the yew was listed as one of the seven great 'Chieftain Trees', and this accolade meant stiff penalties for a person found felling one illegally. The law responded purely to economics, since the tree was valued for its timber, used in 'household vessels, breast plates and other products'.

With its sombre and funereal apearance, it is in more senses than one a tree of death. In all parts except for the fleshy red aril, the plant synthesizes a lethal alkaloid called taxine, a quality not overlooked by enterprising archers during the Middle Ages who dipped the tips of arrows into its juice. Shakespeare was fascinated by these morbid aspects and had Hamlet's uncle poison the king by pouring the juice of yew into his ear.

EUROPEAN YEW

Evergreen

NATIVE TO *Europe*
HEIGHT *15 m (49 ft)*
TRUNK DIAMETER *5.4 m (18 ft)*
TRUNK GIRTH *17 m (56 ft)*
SPREAD *10 m (33 ft)*

ABOVE *The fruits of the yew include lethally poisonous seeds, each encased in a harmless, fleshy red coat, the aril, which is much favoured by birds as a tasty meal.*

LEFT *Impressive scupturing and multiple trunks give more than a hint of the immense age achieved by this colossal specimen of European yew at Tandridge, Surrey, England.*

DESERT TEAK

Tecomella undulata

The desert teak is an altogether different type of tree from the more familiar tropical producer of teak timber, *Tectona grandis*. Desert teak belongs in the jacaranda family of flowering trees and shrubs and is restricted in its native range, as its common name indicates, to dry desert regions of western and northwestern India, where it is now becoming an increasingly endangered species.

Desert teak is also known locally as rohida and marwar teak. It grows chiefly in the hinterland of an immense arid region that forms a natural boundary between India and Pakistan known as the Thar or Great Indian Desert, lying mainly in the state of Rajasthan. In a region where trees of any kind are scarce and hardwood is a valuable commodity not only for construction purposes but also for charcoal production, the species has increasingly fallen victim to unregulated logging and is now an infrequent sight. It is also known from some other desert regions of the Middle East.

A near-evergreen tree that is potentially medium sized, it is slow growing and this, combined with its value for timber means that those in the desert rarely grow to more than 10 metres (33 ft) in height before succumbing to the axe – although, when it is cultivated as an ornamental for its pretty flowers, it can achieve considerably larger dimensions. In the exposed, open desert, it takes on a rather untidy profile, with few upwardly directed branches bearing limited amounts of foliage, which nonetheless provides a scant amount of shade from the fierce summer heat. Leaves are lanceolate with wavy margins, shed briefly and then replaced almost at once in spring, and are regularly browsed by livestock including cattle, camels, sheep and goats at whatever height they are accessible.

The requirements of the desert teak for survival are fairly basic, since it can manage well on stabilized sand dunes with very little rainfall and cope with extremes of daytime and night temperature. It does, however, require a lot of light. The rooting system of the tree is, of necessity, extensive, forming a wide network under the soil surface, an attribute that also makes it a valuable species in the battle against soil erosion.

The flowers are the tree's all-too-brief crowning splendour. They emerge in spring, generally in January and February in company with the fresh leaves, in densely packed clusters or racemes of up to seven flowers. Each bloom unfolds with a big, showy, funnel-shaped corolla, gloriously coloured in yellow, orange and red. The fruit is an elongated, flattened and slightly curved capsule, up to 20 centimetres (8 in) in length, containing winged seeds.

DESERT TEAK

Deciduous (briefly)

NATIVE TO *Northwest India*
HEIGHT *10 m (33 ft)*
TRUNK DIAMETER *0.4 m (1 ft)*
TRUNK GIRTH *1.25 m (4 ft)*
SPREAD *10 m (33 ft)*

ABOVE *Desert teaks dot the arid, flat landscape of the Thar Desert, capable of surviving for months with little or no rainfall.*

LEFT *Related to the jacaranda, a desert teak shows off its all-too-brief floral finery in early spring in the remote Thar Desert of India's northwest.*

WESTERN RED CEDAR

Thuja plicata

The giants of the forest community are all to be found among the more ancient group of cone-bearing trees, the Gymnosperms. A number of species attaining truly massive stature, whether in height, body mass or a combination of both, are included in this book. Western red cedar, native to the Pacific northwest of North America, is not the biggest when set beside such majestic members as the coast redwood and the wellingtonia, but it ranks high on the list, nonetheless.

The common name of this tree is confusing, because it is not a true cedar but rather a member of the cypress family. A stately looking tree, it is borne up on an immense reddish-barked trunk, with boughs that can sweep close to the ground if it is growing in the open with free space around it. A fully mature specimen may reach a height of 70 metres (230 ft) with a trunk diameter of 4 metres (13 ft), wider than a railway carriage. Like several other cone-bearing species it can also achieve considerable longevity, and at least one Canadian veteran has been calculated to have first put out shoots some 1,500 years ago.

Western red cedar prefers life in damp, fertile soils, and is generally found growing in a native coastal range that runs from southwest Canada to the northwest tip of California, and from sea level up to altitudes of about 2,300 metres (7,546 ft). It has also become naturalized in Britain, having been planted first in Argyllshire, Scotland, in 1876, and is extensively cultivated throughout the temperate regions of the globe as a timber-producing tree with excellent resistance to decay. With this property in mind, it was once a favoured material among Native Americans for building their canoes.

The tree mixes readily with Douglas fir and western hemlock in forest communities where, with less space, it tends to develop a narrowly conical crown of short branches, drooping at their extremities, atop a heavily buttressed and tapered trunk. The bark is fibrous and peels away in shreds, and the foliage is of green, flat scales rather than needles. The name *plicata* actually refers to the appearance of the leaves having little folds or creases.

The cones are separately male and female, carried on the same tree, and the males shed their pollen early in the spring. Pollination is by wind, and the female cones are greenish-yellow, ripening to brown. Clustered together and pointing upwards on new stems, each cone is oval, short and consists of up to 12 overlapping cone scales, each bearing up to three winged seeds that are released in the autumn of the same year.

WESTERN RED CEDAR

Evergreen

NATIVE TO *Northwest coast of North America*
HEIGHT *70 m (230 ft)*
TRUNK DIAMETER *4 m (13 ft)*
TRUNK GIRTH *12.5 m (41 ft)*
SPREAD *15 m (49 ft)*

ABOVE *The foliage of the western red cedar takes the form of flattened, green scales.*

LEFT *The massive stature of a mature western red cedar is apparent when looking up the trunk of this giant specimen on the Pacific west coast in British Columbia, Canada.*

SMALL-LEAVED LIME

Tilia cordata

The *Tilia* genus includes some 30 species spread across the temperate regions of the northern hemisphere. Far from being the most commonly encountered these days, *Tilia cordata* is, however, arguably the prettiest. A glorious avenue of the elegant shady trees gave their name to the famous Unter den Linden in Berlin, and it is the national tree of more than one central European country, including the Czech and Slovakian republics.

The native range of the small-leaved lime extends throughout Europe and into western Asia, and from remains found in peat bogs we know that it grew in western Europe and other parts of the continent from shortly after the end of the last Ice Age. Where it is to be found in the wild, it is generally regarded as being an indicator of ancient woodland. The tree is, however, becoming an increasingly rare sight, and these days most of the limes grown in cultivation as ornamentals are a hybrid cross between *Tilia cordata* and a larger-leaved species, *Tilia platyphyllos*. The result of this match is the European lime, *Tilia vulgaris*. Although called 'lime' or 'linden' in Europe, the tree is generally known in North America as 'basswood'.

Small-leaved lime was a popular species for planting in the 17th century and became a favourite subject for landscape painters. One of the most famous collections of the trees in Britain remains those standing in the grounds of Hampton Court Palace, in Surrey, England. The species is known to achieve considerable longevity, and specimen trees have been dated to around 800 years of age. Today, the small-leaved lime is sometimes selected to replace English elms that were lost to catastrophic disease from the early 1970s.

The small-leaved lime is no shrimp. It grows to a statuesque height of some 35 metres (115 ft) with a densely rounded profile, borne up on a sturdy trunk clothed in fibrous greyish bark with shallow vertical seams, and like all limes it is deciduous. The species name *cordata* means 'heart-shaped', and refers to the leaves. These are 5–10 centimetres (2–4 in) long with serrated margins and coloured a pretty delicate green, paler on the underside. One of the latest trees to flower in Europe, in June and July it erupts with masses of scented, pale creamy-white blossoms in clusters borne on long slender 'wings' that curve downwards. The flowers are monoecious, including both male and female parts, chiefly pollinated by bees and are thus important for honey production. The fruit that results from fertilization is a rounded drupe that contains several seeds.

SMALL-LEAVED LIME

Deciduous

NATIVE TO *Europe, western Asia*
HEIGHT *35 m (115 ft)*
TRUNK DIAMETER *2 m (7 ft)*
TRUNK GIRTH *6.25 m (21 ft)*
SPREAD *35 m (115 ft)*

ABOVE *The small delicate flowers that hang from the branch tips in scented, creamy-white clusters make, when dried, a soothing herbal tea.*

LEFT *A snow-bedecked, 500-year-old small-leaved lime, bereft of its foliage, still presents a delightful spectacle in a winter field in frosty Bavaria, Germany.*

LARGE-LEAVED LIME
Tilia platyphyllos

Large-leaved lime occupies a similar native range to its close relative, the small-leaved lime, and is found growing wild across most of Europe, including the southwestern corner of the British Isles. It has also been introduced to parts of North America, where it has gained popularity as an ornamental used to provide attractive shading along urban streets.

There are two chief distinctions between this species and its cousin, *Tilia cordata*. The first, as its name suggests, lies in the much larger size of the leaves that it bears. But it also possesses an advantage for gardeners when grown as an ornamental in that it does not readily produce untidy crops of suckers or side shoots from the trunk base, which are among the less sightly characteristics of both the small-leaved lime and the common hybrid of the two species, the European lime. In common with the small-leaved lime, however, this tree can achieve considerable age. A famous and gnarled veteran known as the Bojnice Linden that stands in the grounds of Bojnice Castle in Slovakia is believed to be at least 700 years old.

A popular tree for planting in parks and larger gardens, large-leaved lime can reach a majestic height of some 40 metres (131 ft) when fully mature, though it is rarely seen at more than 30 metres (98 ft) tall. It grows in a fairly narrowly rounded profile, its stout trunk with grey and finely seamed bark branching into broad, upward-sweeping limbs whose young twigs remain an attractive reddish-brown through their first winter. The deciduous foliage that alternates along the stems takes the form of heart-shaped leaves with serrated edges not unlike those of *Tilia cordata*, but unfolding to a large size, sometimes up to 15 centimetres (6 in) in length. The leaf also differs in that it bears distinctive white down running along the midrib and veins on the underside, while the small-leaved lime carries wholly glabrous foliage. The leaves of lime species never turn russet in autumn, but merely fade to a rather dull yellow.

Large-leaved lime generally flowers roughly two weeks earlier in the year than its small-leaved counterpart, though bearing similar small, creamy-white and strongly scented blossoms, which prove an irresistible midsummer lure to bees. The flowers are arranged in little clusters or cymes that hang from long, pendulous winged bracts and are pollinated by visiting bees. The fruits that develop after fertilization are oval, ribbed drupes that hang in little nut-like clusters and, when freed from the tree, can be carried on the wind for some distance by the winged bract, which serves as a little sail.

LARGE-LEAVED LIME

Deciduous

NATIVE TO *Europe*
HEIGHT *40 m (131 ft)*
TRUNK DIAMETER *3.5 m (11 ft)*
TRUNK GIRTH *11 m (36 ft)*
SPREAD *30 m (98 ft)*

ABOVE *The leaves are heart shaped with serrated edges and, as the common name of the tree suggests, they attain considerable size.*

LEFT *Early winter sun creates magical patterns as it percolates through the fading foliage of a large-leaved lime in Bavaria, Germany.*

EASTERN or CANADIAN HEMLOCK
Tsuga canadensis

Not to be confused with its close relative, the western hemlock, this impressive and long-lived evergreen tree is a native of the eastern side of North America and is one of about ten species of *Tsuga* worldwide. There is no botanical link between the conifer and the herbaceous plant of the same name. However, a distinctive smell is given off by the foliage when it is crushed, which is reminiscent of the odour of the poisonous hemlock.

The native range of eastern hemlock extends from Nova Scotia in the north down the eastern seaboard as far as Alabama, although it does not quite reach into Florida. A member of the pine family, the species tends to be long lived, with the oldest recorded specimen having stood for more than 550 years and not achieving maturity for some 300 years. In exceptional instances, these trees have been known to reach heights of more than 50 metres (164 ft) and the tallest surviving specimen, known as the Noland Mountain Tree, standing in the Great Smoky Mountains National Park, has been measured at just short of 52 metres (171 ft). This qualifies the species as the largest conifer native to the eastern United States, although generally the trees reach a more modest 30 metres (98 ft), developing a tidy, pyramid shape and branches that sweep low to the ground.

Eastern hemlock can be found growing on hillsides at altitudes of up to 1,800 metres (5,906 ft), and it copes well with being shaded by other trees in a forest community. For ideal living conditions, however, it requires a cool, humid climate and soil that is humus rich and regularly moistened but also well drained.

The trunk is clothed with scaly brown bark that becomes deeply seamed in older trees, while the fresh twigs are distinctly downy and more yellowish-brown. The glossy, green foliage takes the form of little flattened, needle-like leaves with blunt tips arranged in spirals on either side of the stems. The inflorescence is small and of insignificant appearance, with male and female borne separately on the same tree. The male catkins appear in the leaf axils and the small female cones are borne in terminal clusters at the ends of stems, at first pale green then becoming brown and ripened in their second year.

Eastern hemlock does not rank as an especially sought-after ornamental tree, although its large size and regular cone shape make it a species that is often planted in parks and large estates. Its value is mainly a commercial one, because although the wood is coarse grained and splinters readily when machined, it is fairly soft, can be pulped and is used extensively in the paper-making industry.

EASTERN HEMLOCK

Evergreen

NATIVE TO *Eastern North America*
HEIGHT *50 m (164 ft)*
TRUNK DIAMETER *1.75 m (6 ft)*
TRUNK GIRTH *5.5 m (18 ft)*
SPREAD *20 m (66 ft)*

ABOVE *A beautiful detail of a burl of gnarly old growth on an eastern hemlock.*

LEFT *The tall, straight trunks of eastern hemlock blend into the mists of an early morning in the Great Smoky Mountains National Park.*

WYCH ELM

Ulmus glabra

There exist some 40 species of elm worldwide, expanded by a considerably larger number of cultivars. Most, but not all, are deciduous and among them wych elm is the single member of the genus that is truly native to Britain and Ireland. It has also proved marginally more resistant to the devastation of Dutch elm disease than some of its counterparts, including *Ulmus procera*, confusingly called the English elm.

Prior to the arrival of a particularly virulent strain of the fungal disease in Europe that ravaged millions of elm trees from the 1970s onwards, wych elm was a common sight, and was much loved as a symbol of the European countryside – if anything, more so than the oak. The name wych elm bears no relation to witches, but is a corruption of the Old English root from which 'wicker' derives. It means 'strong but flexible', and refers to the characteristic properties of elm branches.

The tree often frequents water's edges, and thus the name Loch Lomond derives from the Gaelic meaning 'Lake of the Elms', but it can also be found growing on lower slopes of mountains. The species does not propagate by means of the suckers that characterize most other elms, but by seed, and this may explain how it has managed to avoid, at least in part, the transmission of the deadly fungus.

Where it still survives the devastation, wych elm grows to a substantial size and may occasionally achieve a height of 40 metres (131 ft) or more when fully mature, branching from near the base with upwardly directed limbs to produce a broad, dense-leaved profile. The trunk and boughs are clothed in a smooth, grey bark, from which the name *glabra* ('smooth') comes, since the bark only becomes roughened and fissured in old age. The young stems lack the 'wings' or lengthwise ridges that are seen in other elm species. The foliage is of coarsely roughened large leaves, up to 9 centimetres (4 in) long, pointed at the tips and with serrated margins, borne alternately along the stems with almost no petiole showing.

Elms are generally tricky to distinguish from one another, but an unusual feature of the leaves of wych elm is worthy of close inspection. Like that of almost all other members of the genus, the leaf base is asymmetric, but unlike other species the larger lobe crosses over the short leaf stalk covering it. The flowers appear in early spring. Small and devoid of petals, they consist simply of a mass of pink or red stamens surrounding the female parts and pollination is by wind. The fruit resulting from fertilization is an oval, broad-winged samara containing a single seed at its centre.

WYCH ELM

Deciduous

NATIVE TO *The British Isles*
HEIGHT *40 m (131 ft)*
TRUNK DIAMETER *1.75 m (6 ft)*
TRUNK GIRTH *5.5 m (18 ft)*
SPREAD *30 m (98 ft)*

ABOVE *Developing fruits take the form of broad-winged samaras, each with a single seed at its centre.*

LEFT *The wych elm has largely survived the ravages of Dutch elm disease that have decimated the English elm and remains a true symbol of the European countryside.*

ENGLISH ELM

Ulmus procera

Before the rise of a new and virulent strain of Dutch elm disease in the 1970s, this big, imposing tree was a common sight across the landscape of much of Europe and clothed large parts of the countryside. Today, having succumbed to the onslaught of the lethal fungal parasite, *Ophiostoma ulmi*, it has been virtually wiped out through a large part of its native range.

We should probably treat the common name English elm with a certain amount of reservation, because this tree has never been a native of the British Isles, much less of England. It appears that it was introduced to Britain by the Romans specifically for the purpose of providing a suitable support on which to train their vines, and for this reason it has also been known as the Atinian elm, after the town of Atina in the wine-growing Lazio region of central Italy.

It is a deciduous tree that, at full size, can reach an imposing 40 metres (131 ft) or more in height, with a somewhat narrower profile than its less vulnerable cousin, the wych elm. Although there is some doubt about their precise genetic make-up, two veteran trees at Preston Park, Brighton, known as the 'Preston Twins', are claimed to be the oldest known specimens, dating back roughly 400 years. Sadly, these days most of the trees planted since the 1970s do not live much beyond 25 years before disease takes hold, but an effort is being made to preserve the species by continually propagating new trees from suckers. *Ulmus procera* has also been badly affected in parts of North America.

The leaves of *Ulmus procera* are recognizable by their broad, rather rounded shape, each coming to an abrupt point at the apex and smaller than those of wych elm. The foliage is dark green with serrated or toothed margins and coarse, bristly hairs on the upper surfaces, contrasting with a softer, dense down on the under surfaces. Leaves are arranged alternately on the stems, but the unequal lobes at the base do not overlap the leaf stalk as in wych elm.

The tree is monoecious, with male and female parts contained in the same flower, which appears in the spring before the leaves. Petals are wholly absent, and pollen from the prominent mass of reddish-purple stamens is carried on the wind. Unlike the wych elm, the tree does not produce fertile seed and it is propagated entirely by suckers.

ENGLISH ELM

Deciduous

NATIVE TO *Europe*
HEIGHT *40 m (131 ft)*
TRUNK DIAMETER *2 m (7 ft)*
TRUNK GIRTH *6.25 m (21 ft)*
SPREAD *30 m (98 ft)*

ABOVE *The tiny flowers of the English elm, wholly devoid of petals, consist of reddish-purple exposed stamens whose pollen is readily caught by the wind.*

LEFT *The once familiar sight of a tall, mature English elm has now become a considerable rarity in the European landscape.*

GLOSSARY

Adventitious Arising from an abnormal position on the plant, e.g. an adventitious root arising from the trunk of a tree above ground level as an aerial root.

Aril A brighly coloured fleshy envelope surrounding a seed, found in a few plants including yew.

Axil The angled juncture between a stem and a leaf or its petiole.

Berry A succulent fruit made up of a fleshy pericarp and containing more than one seed.

Bract A small leaf with a comparatively undeveloped blade, in which arises a flower or the stalk of an inflorescence.

Calyx Part of the flower consisting of the sepals that may sometimes be fused together and serves to protect the flower in bud.

Capsule A dry, splitting (or dehiscent) fruit developed from a compound ovary and opening to liberate seeds either by slits or pores.

Carpel The female reproductive organ of a flowering plant, consisting of an ovary containing ovules that become seeds after fertilization.

Catkin A type of inflorescence seen in many trees bearing either male or female reproductive parts, with highly reduced or absent petals, and generally relying on wind for transfer of pollen.

Cone A reproductive structure in which a number of highly modified leaves, appearing as scales, are compacted together on a core or axis and bear the seeds.

Corolla A conspicious part of the flower within the calyx, consisting of petals that may be fused together.

Corymb A type of compound inflorescence in which individual flower stalks grow to approximately the same level to create a cluster.

Cultivar A variety of a plant species developed artificially, either by horticultural grafting or genetic manipulation.

Cyme A type of compound inflorescence that is fairly flat-topped, and in which each branch ends in a flower that opens before those below or to the side of it, starting with the central member.

Deciduous A type of foliage that is shed for a significant period of the year, usually during winter.

Dioecious Flowering plants in which male and female reproductive parts are borne on separate plants.

Drupe A succulent fruit in which the carpel wall or pericarp consists of an outer fleshy layer and a hard, inner layer or 'stone' enclosing a single seed.

Endocarp The inner layer of the wall enclosing a carpel that may become hard and woody to produce a 'stone' or a nut.

Epiphyte A plant attached to another plant, not as a parasite but merely using it as a support.

Evergreen A type of foliage that is not normally shed at regular periods of the year.

Fertilization The penetration of the male gamete into its female counterpart, the ovule, resulting in fusion of nuclei and seed development.

Genus A group of living organisms that consist of a smaller or larger number of similar species.

Glabrous Smooth and free from bristles, hairs or down.

Glaucous The surface of a leaf that is waxy to the feel and often of a bluish-green colour.

Lenticel A small, raised pore, generally elliptical in shape and found in woody stems and permitting exchange of gases.

Monoecious Flowering plants in which male and female reproductive parts are borne on the same plant.

Nut A dry, single-seeded fruit typically having a hard, woody wall.

Ovary The female part of a flower surmounted by the receptive stigma and a connecting tube, the style.

Panicle A type of compound inflorescence made up of often pyramid-shaped, branching clusters of flowers where each cluster is a raceme.

Pedicel The stalk of a single flower.

Peduncle The stalk of a compound flower or inflorescence.

Pericarp The wall of a fertilized ovary consisting of epicarp, mesocarp and endocarp.

Petal One of the parts of the corolla of a flower, usually brightly coloured and conspicuous.

Petiole The stalk of a leaf.

Pinnate A compound leaf type in which smaller component leaflets are arranged on either side of a midrib, sometimes but not always with an additional terminal leaflet.

Pollination The transfer of the male gametes to the receptive part of the female flower, either by wind, insect or occasionally other vectors such as birds.

Pome A false fruit, the greater part of which develops from the receptacle of the flower rather than from the ovary.

Raceme A compound inflorescence that develops as a spike-bearing short-stalked flowers along its axis, the oldest flowers at the base.

Receptacle The apex of a flower stalk on which the flower parts are borne, sometimes becoming enlarged to form the flesh for a false fruit.

Samara A winged, dry, single-seeded fruit. Samaras may be single or double.

Sepal One of the parts forming the calyx of a flower, usually green and leaf like, protecting the young flower in bud, sometimes taking on the role of a petal.

Species The smallest unit of classification generally used for living organisms. The group whose members have the greatest mutual resemblance.

Stamen The male part of a flower, made up of a filament bearing a terminal anther producing the pollen.

Stomata The pores on a leaf or non-woody stem that allow for gas exchange.

Tepal A part of a flower that combines the role of an attractive petal and a protective sepal.

Umbel A type of inflorescence consisting of a number of flowers, each on stalks of similar length and arising from a common point, thus producing an 'umbrella' shape.

INDEX

ACKNOWLEDGEMENTS

p1 ©Daniel Slocum/Getty Images;
2-3 ©Kees Smans/Getty Images;
4 ©TommL/Getty Images;
6-7 ©Goodshoot/Getty Images;
8-9 ©Tom Schwabel;
10 ©Image Source/Corbis;
11 ©Zoran Zivkovic/Getty Images;
12 ©Raquel Nast;
13 ©Maurice Nimmo/FLPA RM;
14 ©Christopher Gallagher/Getty Images;
15 ©Phil McLean/FLPA RM;
17 ©41776.000000/Getty Images;
19 ©Mark Bolton/Getty Images;
19 ©David Davies;
20 ©imagebroker/Alamy;
21 ©M & J Bloomfield/Alamy;
22 ©Visual&Written SL/Alamy;
23 ©Greg Kretovic/Getty Images;
24 ©imagebroker/Alamy;
25 ©iStockphoto/Thinkstock;
27 ©John H Pettigrew/Science Photo Library;
28 ©Wildlife GmbH/Alamy;
29 ©Hemera/Thinkstock;
30 ©hlem/Getty Images;
31 ©Science Photo Library/Alamy;
30 ©Chris Mattison/Alamy;
31 ©Martin Fowler/Alamy;
34 ©Humberto Olarte Cupas/Alamy;
35 ©blickwinkel/Alamy;
36 ©david hancock/Alamy;
37 ©Laurie Wilson/Getty Images;
38 ©Corbis;
39 ©fotolinchen/Getty Images;
40-41 ©Tui De Roy/Minden Pictures/Getty Images;
42 ©Michael Wheatley/Alamy;
43 ©Kevin Ebi/Alamy;
44 ©David Kilpatrick/Alamy;
45 ©Yali Shi/Getty Images;
46 ©Paul Brown/Alamy;
47 ©Kari Marttila/Alamy;
48 ©David Hosking/FLPA;
49 ©Mohammed Abidally/Alamy;
50 ©Bob Gibbons/Alamy;
51 ©Yuriy Brykaylo/Getty Images;
52 ©Phillip Merritt;
53 ©John Nelson;
54 ©Natural Garden Images/Alamy;
55 ©sodapix/Getty Images;
56 ©Oriol Alamany/Alamy;
57 ©Science Photo Library/Alamy;
58 ©Edward Parker/Alamy;
59 ©Christopher Nicholson/Alamy;
60 ©PBPA Paul Beard Photo Agency/Alamy;
61 ©John Glover/Alamy;
62 ©imagebroker/Alamy;
63 ©Scenics & Science/Alamy;
64 ©S.b.m. Hotting/Getty Images;
65 ©Factoryhill/Alamy;
66 ©Anthony Cooper/Science Photo Library;
67 ©Irina Drazowa-Fischer/Getty Images;
68 ©Dr Jeremy Burgess/Science Photo Library;
69 ©David Hosking/FLPA RM;
70 ©David Wall/Alamy;
71 ©F1online digitale Bildagentur GmbH/Alamy;
72 ©Douglas Peebles Photography/Alamy;
73 ©Johan Larson/Getty Images;
74 ©Derek Stone/Getty Images;
75 ©Rudi Tapper/Getty Images;
76 ©Sarah Cuttle/Getty Images;
77 ©mke1963;

78 ©Melburnian;
79 ©Keith Rushforth/FLPA RM;
80 ©Roland Knauer/Alamy;
81 ©Peter Bryant;
82 ©Linda Kennedy/Alamy;
83 ©John Glover/Alamy;
84 ©Florapix/Alamy;
85 ©Fabrice Bettex/Alamy;
86 ©John Ferro Sims/Alamy;
87 ©Bart Wursten;
88 ©Ulrich Doering / Alamy;
89 ©Ray Ives/Getty Images;
90 ©Bill Bachman/Alamy;
91 ©Craig Ingram/Alamy;
92-93 ©Danita Delimont/Alamy;
94 ©brenton west/Alamy;
95 ©blickwinkel/Alamy;
96 ©Arterra Picture Library/Alamy;
97 ©Derek Croucher/Alamy;
98 ©2005 Simon Watson/Botanica;
99 ©blickwinkel/Alamy;
100 ©Aditya "Dicky" Singh/Alamy;
101 ©Shubhada Nikharge;
102 ©Kevin Schafer/Alamy;
103 ©blickwinkel/Alamy;
104 ©FLPA/Alamy;
105 ©MichaelGrantPlants/Alamy;
106 ©STOCKFOLIO®/Alamy;
107 ©blickwinkel/Alamy;
108 ©Frans Lemmens/Getty Images;
109 ©John Warburton-Lee Photography/Alamy;
110 ©Martin Hughes-Jones/Alamy;
111 ©(2008) www.NZPlantPics.com;
112 ©Nigel Hicks/Alamy;
113 © Yvonne Duffe/Alamy;
114 ©Francois Theron/Getty Images;
115 ©Ron Chapple Stock/Getty Images;
116 ©Adrian Davies/Alamy;
117 ©Andrey Nikolajew/Getty Images;
118 ©Edward Parker/Alamy;
119 ©Maximilian Weinzierl/Alamy;
120 ©Botanicum/Alamy;
121 ©blickwinkel/Alamy;
122 ©Tom Mackie/Alamy;
123 ©John Gregory/Alamy;
124 ©Tim Gainey/Alamy;
125 ©Martin Hughes-Jones/Alamy;
126 ©blickwinkel/Alamy;
127 ©Zoonar RF/Getty Images;
128 ©tonyoquias/Getty Images;
129 ©iStockphoto/Thinkstock;
130 ©Bob Sacha/Corbis;
131 ©Wolfgang Kaehler/Corbis;
132 ©Antonio Macias Marin/Getty Images;
133 ©Paolo Cipriani/Getty Images;
134 ©CuboImages srl/Alamy;
135 ©Maximilian Weinzierl/Alamy;
136 ©John Glover/Alamy;
137 ©Design Pics Inc./Alamy;
138 ©Duncan Usher/Alamy;
139 ©Zoonar RF/Getty Images;
140 ©Prisma Bildagentur AG/Alamy;
141 ©Ellen McKnight/Alamy;
142 ©Peter Blottman/Alamy;
143 ©LindaJoHeilman/ Getty Images;
144 ©Kip Evans/Alamy;
145 ©Emmanuel Rondeau/Alamy;
146 ©blickwinkel/Alamy;
147 ©Arterra Picture Library/Alamy;
148 ©Sanibel-Captiva Conservation Foundation;

149 ©Doug Meikle/Getty Images;
150 ©Ross Jolliffe/Alamy;
151 ©Val Duncan/Kenebec Images/Alamy;
152 ©guichaoua/Alamy;
153 ©Purple Marbles Madeira/Alamy;
154 ©Edward Parker/Alamy;
155 ©GFK-Flora/Alamy;
156 ©Mike Grandmaison/All Canada Photos/Corbis;
157 ©blickwinkel/Alamy;
158 ©CuboImages srl/Alamy;
159 ©Bob Gibbons/Alamy;
160-161 ©Jon Mullen/Alamy;
162 ©Prisma Bildagentur AG/Alamy;
163 ©blickwinkel/Alamy;
164 ©blickwinkel/Alamy;
165 ©iStockphoto/Thinkstock;
166 ©Terry Donnelly/Alamy;
167 ©M & J Bloomfield/Alamy;
168 ©Nature Picture Library/Alamy;
169 ©Science Photo Library/Alamy;
170 ©Stephen Spraggon/Alamy;
171 ©iStockphoto/Thinkstock;
172 ©RWP/Alamy;
173 ©altrendo nature/Getty Images;
174 ©Luisa Amare/Shutterstock;
175 ©Chris Mattison/Alamy;
176 ©Brian Hoffman/Alamy;
177 ©Susanne Masters/Alamy;
178 ©Mary H. Swift/Alamy;
179 ©Maksimchuk Vitaly/ Getty Images;
180 ©Arterra Picture Library/Alamy;
181 ©flowerphotos/Alamy;
182 ©Informasi Tanaman Kehutanan;
183 ©Martin Siepmann/Corbis;
184 ©Bart Wursten;
185 ©Nicholas Poulos;
186 ©Corbis Nomad/Alamy;
187 ©Christina Bollen/Alamy;
188-189 ©Prisma Bildagentur AG/Alamy;
190 ©Danita Delimont/Alamy;
191 ©Wildlife GmbH/Alamy;
192 ©FLPA/Alamy;
193 ©altrendo nature/Stockbyte/Thinkstock;
194 ©altrendo nature/Getty Images;
195 ©Photoshot/Alamy;
196 ©Douglas Peebles/Corbis;
197 ©Stan Osolinski/Getty Images;
198 ©blickwinkel/Alamy;
199 ©iStockphoto ID123083114/ Thinkstock;
200 ©Mark Conlin/Alamy;
201 ©James Randklev/Getty Images;
202-203 ©Clint Farlinger/Alamy;
204 ©Archie Miles/Alamy;
205 ©Andrzej Tokarski/Getty Images;
206 ©Hadi Karimi;
207 ©Bart Nedobre/Alamy;
208 ©Gunter Marx/Alamy;
209 ©Purestock/Alamy;
210 ©blickwinkel/Alamy;
211 ©hsvrs/Getty Images;
212 ©blickwinkel/Alamy;
213 ©blickwinkel/Alamy;
214 ©Steve Satushek/Getty Images;
215 ©altrendo nature/Getty Images;
216 ©Science Photo Library/Alamy;
217 ©Brian & Sophia Fuller/Alamy;
218 ©David Hosking/Alamy;
219 ©Simon Colmer and Abby Rex/Alamy;
220 ©Tatiana Boyle/Alamy.

Quercus Editions Ltd
55 Baker Street
7th Floor, South Block
London
W1U 8EW

First published in 2012

© 2012 Quercus Editions Ltd

Design, picture research, and editorial by The Urban Ant Ltd, London [www.theurbanant.com]

A catalogue record of this book is available from the British Library

UK and associated territories:
ISBN 978 1 78087 326 8

Canada: ISBN 978 1 84866 203 2

Manufactured in China

10 9 8 7 6 5 4 3 2 1